The Connected School

The Connected School

TECHNOLOGY AND LEARNING IN HIGH SCHOOL

Barbara Means
William R. Penuel
Christine Padilla
Center for Technology in Learning
SRI International

JOSSEY-BASS
A Wiley Company
www.josseybass.com

Published by

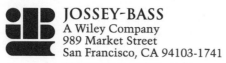

JOSSEY-BASS
A Wiley Company
989 Market Street
San Francisco, CA 94103-1741

www.josseybass.com

Jossey-Bass books and products are available through most bookstores. To contact Jossey-Bass directly, call (888) 378-2537, fax to (800) 605-2665, or visit our website at www.josseybass.com.

Substantial discounts on bulk quantities of Jossey-Bass books are available to corporations, professional associations, and other organizations. For details and discount information, contact the special sales department at Jossey-Bass.

We at Jossey-Bass strive to use the most environmentally sensitive paper stocks available to us. Our publications are printed on acid-free recycled stock whenever possible, and our paper always meets or exceeds minimum GPO and EPA requirements.

Library of Congress Cataloging-in-Publication Data

Means, Barbara, 1949-
 The connected school : technology and learning in high school /
Barbara Means, William R. Penuel, and Christine Padilla.
    p. cm. — (The Jossey-Bass education series)
Includes bibliographical references and index.
 ISBN 0-7879-5953-7 (alk. paper)
 1. Educational technology—United States—Case studies. 2.
Education, Secondary—United States—Case studies. 3.
Computer-assisted instruction—United States—Case studies. I.
Title: Technology and learning in high school. II. Penuel, William R.,
1970- III. Padilla, Christine. IV. Title. V. Series.
 LB1028.3 .M413 2001
 373.1'334—dc21
                                                          2001004678

HB Printing   10 9 8 7 6 5 4 3 2 1

The Jossey-Bass Education Series

Sponsored by SRI International

Funded by The Joyce Foundation
Chicago, IL

Contents

Preface

Background

Education reformers have found that secondary schools are more difficult to change profoundly than their elementary counterparts. Strictures and stakes associated with earning a diploma and gaining acceptance into college, the departmental structure, and the sheer size of their staffs and student bodies all make high schools resistant to change. When we studied technology's role in supporting education reform in the early 1990s, most of our nine cases involved elementary and middle schools. The single radically altered technology-supported high school in our study was a school-within-a-school. Although technology resources were much more widely available in the late 1990s than at the time of our earlier study, there was little indication of widespread use of technology in high school classrooms in ways that would support an educational reform agenda. We wanted to see if we could find secondary schools where technology was being used to support more student-centered forms of instruction, deeper involvement with content, more collaboration, and more complex assignments.

By the late 1990s the student-to-computer ratio for schools serving large proportions of low-income students was nearing that for schools in general. Large differences still existed, however, in terms of Internet access at both the school and classroom levels. When we began our fieldwork the telecommunications discount for schools, the so-called E-rate, was just coming into effect, with schools and districts working on technology plans so that they could qualify for the discounts. Although some districts had vigorously pursued the districtwide implementation of technology in the middle and late 1980s, most urban districts had not. Those schools within these districts that were heavy technology users were pioneers, some years ahead of most district schools in terms of dealing with issues surrounding technology infrastructure, developing a vision for technology's role in the core curriculum, identifying relevant technology-based content resources, and providing teacher training and support. We sought such schools for study in the hope that their experiences and strategies would provide both inspiration and concrete ideas for the much larger number of high schools following in their wake. We also included several schools at an earlier stage in their technology implementation efforts. These schools are struggling with the choices and trade-offs the technology pioneers have already made. By examining issues of technology integration within urban high schools, we hoped to shed light on the challenges these schools and their districts face that complicate the already difficult process of technology integration. We sought to find the stories behind the statistics. Why are technology uses other than skills remediation relatively infrequent in urban high schools? What kinds of leadership and support are in place in schools that defy the stereotype?

Overview of Contents

This book opens with a chapter discussing issues of technology access that have come to be called the "digital divide." We argue that, though important, differences between schools serving larger and smaller proportions of low-income students in terms of network connections and computers per se are only the tip of the iceberg with respect to inequality of educational experience. Technology can be used in many very different ways. Some technology-based systems are designed to support the conventional segmenting (some would say fragmentation) of the curriculum and emphasize factual

knowledge and narrowly defined skills. Other uses provide interesting digital resources and invite exploration—but sometimes without enough structure to lead students to discover the important
concepts, relationships, or data patterns in the provided material.
Software that structures and supports student engagement with rep-
resentations of important concepts and complex systems is available, albeit often through offerings of universities or nonprofit R&D
centers rather than commercial entities (see Roschelle, Pea, Hoadley,
Gordin, & Means, 2000 for a description of some of the better-
designed learning software). Still other classroom approaches to technology integration involve students in using general-purpose
technology tools in much the same way that practitioners of many
professions do in their work. We group these latter two instructional
uses of technology together and refer to them as "student empow-
ering." The distinction between these and other uses is that students are being primed to think and create *with* technology rather
than learning *from* technology. Such uses are sometimes referred to
as "constructivist" or "reform-oriented." Available data suggest that
student-empowering uses of technology are more common in schools
serving suburban, higher-income, and high-achieving students than
in urban and low-income schools. This chapter then describes the
nature of our fieldwork—our search for student-empowering uses of
technology—at six urban public high schools, three each in Detroit
and Chicago.

Each of the six chapters that follow describes one of the high
schools. Chapter Two provides a portrait of a general high school
located within an economically stressed urban Empowerment Zone.
Thanks to the efforts of the school's leadership and to state and federal compensatory education programs and private philanthropy,
the school has had the funding to obtain an impressive technology
inventory. At the time of our fieldwork, the central challenge fac-
ing the school was putting that inventory to good use—providing
an instructional vision, training, and support for teachers. The
school's teachers were not only unaccustomed to using technologies
themselves for the most part but also represented a wide array of

viewpoints concerning instructional goals and methods appropriate for their students. Chapter Three moves to a Chicago high school with an explicit vocational orientation. The school seeks to use technology as a lure for attracting students from across the district. The school has been "out in front" of districtwide technology implementation efforts, building its infrastructure and programs through partnerships with the private sector and by seeking grant funds for its activities.

The fourth chapter tells the story of a Chicago options school with a mathematics and science focus. Although the school has vigorously implemented technology to support its academic program, it views technology as just one of the prerequisites for the rigorous academic program it embraces. The climate of mutual support among teachers and organizational supports for teacher collaboration are key aspects of the school's technology implementation strategy. Chapter Five describes a small, alternative high school that, thanks to corporate philanthropy and staff initiative, was one of the first Chicago schools to have Internet access in most of its instructional rooms.

Chapter Six describes another small high school, in this case a selective, traditionally academic Detroit high school that has been lauded as one of the nation's strongest public high schools. The school's struggle to introduce technology at a meaningful level makes it clear that technology implementation is still far from a routine part of high school planning and activity. Chapter Seven describes activities at a high school that has served as a technology demonstration center for Detroit. Much of the technology-based activity in this school occurs in its Tech Center, run by an enterprising technology coordinator and by the students themselves.

Finally, in Chapter Eight we provide a summary of issues raised by the cases as a whole. We begin by examining the barriers to implementing student-empowering uses of technology that were observed across the six urban high schools. To provide a baseline for comparison, brief descriptions of technology use and support in two suburban high schools in communities outside Detroit and Chicago are described. We contrast characteristics of these schools and their districts with their urban counterparts to try to distinguish between aspects of technology implementation that are problematic for any school and those that are particularly challenging in city schools and districts. Finally, we offer recommendations for district administrators, school leaders, and teachers regarding what they can do to foster technology implementation and student-empowering uses of technology.

Acknowledgments

The efforts of many people went into making this book possible. A grant from the Joyce Foundation supported both the field studies on which the book is based and manuscript preparation. Particular thanks go to our project officer, Peter Mich, who not only helped us conceive the design of the study but also introduced us to key informants. The study would not have been possible without input and support from the district offices. Richard White, the Director of Learning Technology for the Chicago Public Schools, and Juanita Clay-Chambers, Associate Superintendent for Educational Services within the Detroit Public Schools, were extremely generous with their time and their insights. At the school level, we are indebted to more staff members and students than we can name. Their willingness to welcome us into their classrooms and to share their perspectives, triumphs, and frustrations enables us to tell their stories. Special thanks are due to our chief contact at each school: Claudia Burton, Mumford High School; Tom and Kathy Daniels, Best Practice High School; Katie Fitzner, Murray-Wright High School; Richard Gazda, Von Steuben Metropolitan Science Center; Phil Lampi, Renaissance High School; and Linda Pierchalski, Bogan Computer Technical High School.

In addition to the authors, SRI researchers Kara Finnegan, Christine Korbak, Ray McGhee, Judi Powell, and Lori Riehl ably conducted the fieldwork on which this book is based. Lesley Iura, senior education editor at Jossey-Bass, provided encouragement starting from the time when the project was still at the idea stage.

And finally, I am grateful to my support system on the home front. Thanks to Dick for being there every step of the way, but especially for urging me to get the last piece finished and to part with the manuscript. And thanks to Annie who represents the generation growing up with all this new technology and who was so forbearing when Mom needed to work on her book instead of playing Pokémon.

Barbara Means
Menlo Park, CA
March 2001

The Authors

Barbara Means directs the Center for Technology in Learning at SRI International, an independent nonprofit research organization based in Menlo Park, California. Means is an educational psychologist whose research focuses on ways to foster students' learning of advanced skills and the changes in practice at the school and classroom levels associated with the introduction of technology-supported innovations. She has led numerous research projects concerned with the design, implementation, and evaluation of technology-enhanced approaches to education reform. In addition to the case studies of technology use in urban high schools described in this volume, her recent work includes formulation of an educational technology research agenda for the U.S. Department of Education and the evaluation of GLOBE, an Internet-supported environmental science and education project involving thousands of schools worldwide. Means also codirects (with John Bransford) the assessment research team of the Center for Innovative Learning Technologies (http://www.cilt.org), a center funded by the National Science Foundation with the mission of improving K–16 science and mathematics education.

Means recently served on the National Academy of Sciences' Committee on Developments in the Science of Learning, which produced the volume *How People Learn*. She is currently a member of the Academy's Board on Testing and Assessment (BOTA). Her published works include the edited volumes *Technology and Education Reform* and *Teaching Advanced Skills to At-Risk Students* (with Carol Chelemer and Michael Knapp) and *Comparative Studies of How People Think* (with Michael Cole). Means earned her A.B. in psychology from Stanford University and her Ph.D. in education and intellectual development at the University of California, Berkeley.

William R. Penuel is a senior educational researcher at the Center for Technology in Learning at SRI International. Penuel is a developmental psychologist whose research focuses on measuring student learning in technology-rich school and after-school settings. He has led projects focused on the design of Internet-based assessments, as well as the evaluation of large-scale technology-supported school reforms. His recent work includes the design of handheld-computer assessments of student collaboration for the U.S. Department of Education, and the evaluation of the Challenge 2000 Multimedia Project, one of two technology initiatives recognized as exemplary by a U.S. Department of Education–sponsored national panel of experts in educational technology. Penuel also leads a team of researchers at SRI conducting the evaluation of the U.S. Department of Education's Community Technology Centers program.

Penuel earned his Ed.M. in human development from Harvard University and his Ph.D. in developmental psychology at Clark University in Worcester, Massachusetts.

Christine Padilla is the assistant director of SRI's Center for Education and Human Services. She has worked for more than twenty years in the areas of program evaluation and policy analysis for the improvement of education, especially for disadvantaged students. Currently she is codirecting a series of evaluations and studies of educational technology for the U.S. Department of Education. This work will provide policymakers and practitioners with valuable information on a variety of topics associated with educational technology: teacher professional development models, evaluation approaches at the state and district levels, the digital divide, the status of state and local planning efforts, and how technology is used and supported in schools and classrooms.

The Connected School

Introduction

Technology, Equity, and School Reform

The head of the math department guides us through the halls of an urban high school, known for its high academic standards and focus on preparing minority students for competitive colleges and universities. We stop in at an environmental science class, where the veteran teacher enthusiastically describes their participation in the Rouge River Project. Her students, like those in dozens of other schools in the Detroit area, collected water samples and computed a water quality index during the second week of May. She describes how students at multiple schools have been working with university scientists to monitor all branches of the Rouge River since 1989. Unlike students at other schools, however, her class will not be posting their data on the World Wide Web and examining the data other schools have displayed there. "We don't have the Internet connection."

A few hundred miles away, in a well-to-do Chicago suburb, high school students peruse the home page for their physics class. It invites them to check out the on-line "physics classroom" of instructional pages written in easy-to-understand terms or the multimedia physics studios, with GIF animations and QuickTime movies illustrating physics principles. The virtual "Quiz Room" features quizzes given in the course in past years as well as tips for studying for this year's quizzes. The on-line "Laboratory" features makeup labs for anyone who missed a class lab, and the "Refrigerator" Web page features exemplary student problem solutions.

Data gathered by the U.S. Department of Education and others have documented what has come to be known as the "digital divide." As far back as 1983, observers noted with alarm that technology appeared to be on a road toward doing more to exacerbate differences in educational opportunity than to overcome them (Anderson, Welch, & Harris, 1984). The proportion of wealthy schools with microcomputers was four times that of poor schools with such equipment. By 1994–95, strides toward narrowing the gap in computer access had been made. The average number of students per computer was 11 in schools serving predominantly low-income students compared with 9.5 in those serving the most economically privileged student bodies. More recently, the density of computers in schools serving low-income students appears to be quite similar to that of schools serving average and high-income students (Anderson & Ronnkvist, 1999).

Differences persist in the quality of most of the computers in the two sets of schools, however, and in the amount and diversity of software present. For example, Quality Education Data (QED) technology inventory data for the 1996–97 school year indicated that more than three-quarters of computers in Detroit public schools and nearly half of those in Chicago public school classrooms were older models, most of which could not run current versions of spreadsheet or database programs (Education Writers of America, 1999).

Even larger differences are found in Internet access. In 1998 only 39 percent of classrooms serving the poorest students had Internet access compared with 62 percent of classrooms in schools with the most economically privileged students (National Center for Education Statistics [NCES], 2000). Moreover, students attending schools in middle- or upper-income zip code areas are twice as likely as those in low-income zip codes to have high-speed access to the Internet at school, according to a 1998 survey (Anderson & Ronnkvist, 1999). Becker (2000) has examined the proportion of schools that meet various criteria for a strong technology infrastructure (e.g., 50 percent of computers local area network (LAN)-connected; fewer than twelve students per Internet-connected computer; high-speed Internet access). Schools with more than 40 percent of their students eligible for compensatory education funds were less likely than other schools to meet these criteria. Similarly, the most recent NCES data on Internet access indicate that in 1999 there were seven students per computer with Internet access in the lowest-poverty schools compared with sixteen students per Internet-accessible computer in the highest-poverty schools (NCES, 2000). Thus, no matter which data source or criterion for Internet access we examine, there are significant differences between schools serving students from low-income versus higher-income families.

Finally, even when an adequate technology infrastructure is in place, available survey data suggest that teachers in low-income and urban schools do not use it in the same way teachers do in more affluent settings. In his 1998 national survey Becker (2000) found that teachers in high-poverty elementary and middle schools are more likely to report "remediation of skills" and "mastering skills just taught" as the purposes for which they have their students use computers. By high school, teachers in high-poverty schools view technology as an opportunity for their students to work independently. Becker contrasts the technology uses of teachers in schools with many low-income students with those of teachers with more affluent students: "teachers in high-SES schools [in contrast to those in low-SES schools] were more likely to use computers to teach students skills such as written expression, making presentations to an audience, and analyzing information" (p. 55). Becker attributes these differences in practice to differences in teacher beliefs: "Computer use in low-SES schools often involved very traditional practices and beliefs about student learning, whereas computer use in high-SES schools often reflected more constructivist and innovative teaching strategies" (p. 55).

Federal compensatory education programs have had *mixed* effects with respect to equity. On the one hand, an estimated $2 billion of Title I funds have supported educational technology within schools serving low-income students over the last decade (President's Committee of Advisors on Science and Technology, 1997). On the other hand, compensatory education dollars going to technology at the local level tend to be used for drill and practice in basic skills to the exclusion of the kinds of activities Becker refers to as "more constructivist, intellectual purposes."

Conceptual Framework: Student-Empowering Uses of Technology

In schools serving mostly middle-class students, there is an emphasis on teaching students to think and create *with* technology rather than on simply learning *from* technology. Instruction for middle-class students is geared toward putting the students in control, whereas instruction for low-income students is more likely to put the technology in control (through uses such as delivering information or basic skills practice sessions).

The student-controlled activities more typical in middle-class schools include such things as having students gather and analyze information, produce on-line reports and multimedia presentations of their research findings, manipulate computer models and simulations (or even produce their own models) as they develop and refine their understanding of systems and concepts, and interact with distant scientists as they participate in real scientific expeditions and investigations.

This is not to say that teachers working with low-income students in urban settings never have their students use technology in these ways, and we set out to look for examples of this kind of technology-supported teaching and learning at our urban case study school sites. More specifically, we selected those classes to observe most frequently that contained elements of what we have come to call *student-empowering technology use*. Our concept of student-empowering technology use contains the following six features. It

- emulates the ways in which professionals use technology,
- involves complex tasks,
- requires significant amounts of time for completion,
- gives students latitude in designing their own products and in determining when and how to use technology,
- involves multiple academic disciplines, and
- provides opportunities for student collaboration with peers and outside experts.

Unlike the technology-controlled experiences of learning factual knowledge through computer tutorials or practicing discrete skills on a computer, student-empowering technology uses put the student in a decision-making role, much as professional designers, scientists, journalists, and e-traders use technologies that serve their ends. Because the tasks that students accomplish with technology supports are complex and realistic, they typically call upon knowledge and skill from more than one academic discipline (e.g., scientific understanding, statistical analysis, and writing skills) as well as the ability to use technology skills. The multifaceted nature and high level of challenge posed by these tasks also encourage collaboration among students (who may produce a joint product or simply advise each other or share resources) and with individuals outside the school, who may provide information, suggest interesting problems to solve, act as coaches, or simply serve as an external audience for student work.

Such uses of technology are consistent with contemporary learning theory (see National Research Council, 1999) and with the qualities promoted by educational reformers (see Means, 1994). They foreshadow the environments that knowledge workers will encounter in the next century.

Survey statistics provide an outline of the differences in technology use in different kinds of schools. Wenglinsky (1998), for example, reports that eighth graders who attend urban public schools or who are eligible for free or reduced-priced school lunches are less likely than other eighth graders to have math teachers who use computers primarily for simulations and applications. In this book, we seek to paint the picture behind the numbers. Beyond mere counts of self-reported types of software use, what does the teaching and learning supported by technology look like in urban schools? How is it different from that in more affluent suburban schools? Is technology inevitably a magnifier of educational inequality? What barriers do urban schools have to overcome? Are there urban schools using technology in ways that empower students? If so, how do they do it? What would it take for other urban schools to emulate their strategies?

The Joyce Foundation funded SRI International's Center for Technology in Learning to address these questions through case studies of selected urban high schools' use of technology. This volume presents selected findings from fieldwork conducted primarily during 1998 and 1999 in the Chicago Public Schools (CPS) and the Detroit Public Schools (DPS).

Study Context: Chicago and Detroit Public Schools

Both the Detroit and the Chicago districts serve student populations with significant educational needs. The proportion of the student body eligible for free or subsidized lunches is 83 percent in Chicago and 84 percent in Detroit. In Chicago 54 percent of students are African American and 33 percent Latino; in Detroit 86 percent are African American and 9 percent other racial or ethnic minorities. Just under one-third of Detroit's eleventh-grade students met or exceeded state standards in reading, and 19 percent met or exceeded standards in math in 1998. Among CPS high school students, just 29 percent were reading at or above the national norm and just 31 percent were performing at or above the national norm in mathematics in 1997–98. In Chicago the graduation rate, computed as the number of high school graduates divided by the number of students who entered high school four years earlier (thus including "late graduates" in the numerator), is 65 percent. Coming predominantly from low-income, minority families, CPS and DPS students are much less likely than students in more affluent settings to have significant experience with, and access to, technology in their homes.

With 585 schools and more than 430,000 students, Chicago is the third largest school district in the United States and site of one of the country's most far-reaching efforts in school reform. Passed in 1988, the Chicago School Reform Act gave local school councils unprecedented control over local budgets and hiring and firing in return for accountability—requirements for bringing student achievement test scores in line with state averages under threat of "takeover" by outside organizations. In Chicago, local school councils not only hire principals but also evaluate their performance and have decision-making power over whether or not to renew their contracts. Principals, in turn, can hire teachers as they see fit, without respect to seniority within the district. Another unusual feature of the Chicago Reform is that principals and school councils control significant discretionary budgets, an average of $850,000 at the high school level (Hess, 1999). In 1996 a second piece of state legislation aimed at Chicago schools put the schools under the control of Chicago's mayor, who in turn appointed a chief executive officer (CEO) to run the schools. Under the current plan, schools where fewer than 15 percent of students perform at or above national norms on state-mandated tests are put on probation and then reconstituted with a new staff if improvement is not forthcoming.

Compared with Chicago, Detroit is a somewhat smaller school district seeking to get on the reform path that Chicago pioneered. In the year immediately preceding our case studies, the DPS came under increasing criticism for poor performance and excessive bureaucracy. A 1998 report from an outside consulting firm cited costly and ineffective services and an excess of staff at the district level. The district moved to transfer functions and employees from the central office to twenty "constellations," each composed of a comprehensive high school and its feeder middle and elementary schools along with associated adult and alternative programs (Keller, 1998). The district moves did not satisfy Michigan's governor, however, who pushed state lawmakers to pass a bill early in 1999 putting the city's schools under direct control of the mayor, as part of a "Chicago-style reform."

The emphasis on site-based control within these two districts has implications for the way in which technology gets introduced and supported within their schools. At the time of our research, the Chicago and Detroit district offices had neither the budget, nor the staff, nor the mandate to institute technology planning, purchasing, and support in these reorganized districts in the way districts have in some other parts of the country (e.g., Honey, Carrigg, & Hawkins, 1998). Geraldine Carroll, the head of Detroit's Educational Technology Office describes the shift in positive terms, "The old paradigm of every school receiving uniform support and direction from the central office has been replaced with a more customized presentation of services to fit the unique needs of each school." Under this new paradigm technology does or does not get introduced into individual schools at the option of that school's principal and local council. The commitment, technology savvy, and organizational skills of the principal are even more than usual critical factors in determining the success of technology introduction under site-based management.

A second major characteristic affecting technology implementation in these districts is the strong emphasis on accountability as measured through performance on statewide tests. Although schools have been feeling pressure to modernize their programs and introduce technology, their first requirement is to ensure that their students demonstrate an acceptable level of performance on these state and district examinations. Given the focus of many standardized tests on basic skills and knowledge of discrete facts, accountability programs can reduce administrator and teacher willingness to invest time and effort in student-centered uses of technology to develop advanced skills and conceptual understanding that are not measured on the high-stakes tests.

Technology Infrastructure in the Two Districts

In terms of technology implementation the two districts were at different stages at the time of our study. The CPS established a Department of Learning Technologies independent of the Department of Information Technology Services (ITS) early in 1996. (Previously, ITS was responsible for both administrative and academic computing.) The reorganization gave greater visibility to academic issues surrounding the use of technology. In 1999 Learning Technologies was promoted to "office" status within CPS, with Richard White, the Learning Technologies Officer, reporting directly to Cozette Buckney, the district's Chief Education Officer.

Starting in 1996, the district undertook several major efforts to support technology implementation in Chicago schools. First, a major effort to provide training and technical support around the use of technology was launched. A Technology Resource Network (TRN), consisting of twenty-six individuals designated to act as technology coordinators and teacher trainers, was established. Each school was assigned to a TRN coordinator who could provide training at the site, help the school develop a technology plan, and provide an additional communications link between the school and CPS Learning Technologies. Teacher training offered by the TRNs is supplemented by other forms and sources of professional development. A districtwide technology training day held each October has been characterized as the largest teacher technology training session in the world. An Instructional Intranet offers resources for teachers, including information about standards and detailed lesson plans (Greene, David, & Young, 2000). A summer institute fosters development of technology-supported curriculum units for teachers from twenty-nine pilot schools participating in the Technology Infusion Planning (TIP) program. CPS also supports the University of Chicago's summer Web Institute for Teachers, offered as part of the Chicago University Internet Project (CUIP) for schools in the Hyde Park area. In summarizing these activities, CPS Learning Technologies Officer Richard White asserts that Chicago's professional development with respect to technology integration is ahead of its infrastructure. By providing the teacher training early, the district fostered interest in technology use at the school level.

A second thrust in the CPS technology effort was districtwide planning for a uniform technology structure that would be implemented in all schools. The school board made a commitment to providing all CPS schools with high-speed T-1 access to the Internet plus a router, server, and uninterrupted power supply. Schools would connect to the district's wide area network (WAN) through five administrative drops placed in each school. The CPS technology plan calls for this "Short Scope" phase to be followed by a second stage in which each school would receive connections for their library, computer lab, and ten classrooms. The first stage of this infrastructure plan was completed in the fall of 1999. CPS plans to install the local area network configuration in every school by 2004.

Finally, CPS aggressively pursued maximization of the district's ability to take advantage of the E-rate discounts. The federal Telecommunications Act of 1996 provides for discounts of 20–90 percent (depending on the proportion of low-income students in a school or district) on Internet and intranet connectivity, classroom data cabling, and telecommunications services. While E-rate subsidies cannot be applied to teacher training costs or hardware and software purchases, the CPS viewed the federal program as an opportunity to support a technology infrastructure development that had lagged behind much of the country because of the high costs of upgrading electrical wiring and providing a technology backbone within the district's aging school buildings. In addition to the E-rate application submitted through the district, individual schools were encouraged to get state-approved technology plans so that they could make their own school-level applications and receive subsidies through the program. In a spring 1999 survey of Chicago high schools by The Chicago Panel, half of the schools reported having submitted individual E-rate applications (The Chicago Panel, 1999). In the first year of E-rate funding, Chicago received $49 million, the third largest allocation in the nation. (This figure includes the allocations for 117 Chicago schools that made their own E-rate applications.) These funds supported completion of the Short Scope phase of the district's technology plan in the fall of 1999. In the second round of funding, Chicago garnered $85 million in discounts, the largest allocation to any school district in the nation (The Chicago Panel, 1999).

Although it would not qualify as one of the first districts in the United States to push educational technology implementation, the CPS actions since 1996 have been vigorous and demonstrate a strong commitment to promoting technology use. Nevertheless, from the school perspective, district support only goes so far. With each TRN coordinator assigned to cover twenty-three schools, no single school can expect extensive on-site assistance or training for the district. Similarly, although the district undertook a significant expense in taking on the bill for installing T-1 connections to the schools, individual schools still faced responsibility for connecting the data cabling from the main distribution frame (MDF) room to their computer labs or classrooms with the associated costs of asbestos abatement, electrical upgrades, and within-school wiring as well as the expense of computers and software. In the case of many of Chicago's older, decaying school buildings (nearly half of the district's schools are over fifty years old), these costs were daunting. Recognizing these problems, CPS has established a Local School Education Network program to help schools pay for internal wiring and local area networks. This $57 million fund is intended to ensure that all CPS schools meet a minimum technology standard, with libraries, computer labs, and at least ten instructional classrooms connected to the school network (Honey & Culp, 2000). The CPS Financial Support Services (FINSS) program, a partnership between CPS Learning Technologies and Finance Departments, provides an option to pool five years of allowable discretionary funds to purchase hardware and software (The Chicago Panel, 1999).

Detroit has faced similar challenges of decaying buildings, inadequate wiring, and uncertainties regarding the best organizational home for instructional technology. Up until 1996, only a small minority of Detroit schools had Internet connections of any kind; the district's administrative network supported only dial-up modem access, and few classrooms had connections to the Internet (Honey & Culp, 2000). The district's share of the settlement of a Michigan State lawsuit against Ameritech, received in 1996, enabled DPS to build networks in several high schools. With the advent of E-rate funds, Detroit was able to commit to wiring all of the district's schools, beginning with high schools and middle schools in 1998. Wiring efforts have been complicated, however, by asbestos abatement requirements and by the fact that the telephone cabling in some schools was too old to carry computer signals (Education Writers of America, 1999). A state-level fund has provided $12 million dollars for electrical upgrades in Detroit schools (Honey & Culp, 2000).

As in Chicago, the DPS have reorganized the way in which the district supports technology use in schools. District-level educational technology services began as part of the Division of Educational Services and have maintained a strong emphasis on curriculum integration. At one time, the DPS maintained a Software Department that approved all instructional software. Schools could not use a piece of software until it had been vetted by this office. As the number of computers in schools grew, however, and the need for technical support and computer repair and maintenance rose, educational technology was made part of Information Services. By 1998 the professional development and curriculum integration functions related to technology had once again been made a part of Educational Services, with purchasing and repair of computers remaining with Information Services. In school year 1998–99 Detroit's Educational Technology

Office within Educational Services had twelve technology consultants responsible for providing professional development related to technology use for 280 schools. Information Services had fourteen technicians available to respond to schools' needs for technology maintenance. In 2000 the district announced its intention to out-source technology maintenance entirely. As in Chicago, individual schools in Detroit have had to cover the costs for computer equipment, maintenance, and upgrades out of their own discretionary budgets. With little certainty concerning school budgets from year to year, the ongoing investment required for technology was regarded by many principals as a risky undertaking.

The 1998 DPS E-rate application stated that only one out of eight classrooms in the district was connected to the Internet. Detroit received $15 million from the first round of E-rate funding and about the same amount in the second round. Detroit's E-rate application was managed by the Office of Information Services but required coordination with the Educational Technology Office. A former DPS Director of Information Technology has been quoted as referring to Detroit's early E-rate subsidies as "a godsend" (Honey & Culp, 2000), but they were considerably less than those received by other comparably sized urban districts (Education Writers of America, 1999).

Prior to the E-rate, the DPS approach was to put technology into a school's office, labs, and library, "usually based on school or district politics," according to a former Information Services administrator. The E-rate is making it possible for Detroit schools to bring technology into instructional classrooms, and the E-rate discount formula means that schools serving more low-income students are getting technology first. In all cases, schools still face the problem of finding resources to pay for computers and software. Schools are largely left to fend for themselves in this regard, by using their own discretionary funds or finding corporate donors or securing grants.

The academic side of technology in DPS is the responsibility not of Information Technology but of the Educational Technology

Office within Educational Services. A distinctive feature of the DPS Educational Technology Office is its emphasis on integrating technology use with curriculum. In-service courses cover topics such as "Software in Social Studies" or "Spreadsheets in Science," rather than the more generic technology training (e.g., "Building Web Pages") emphasized in many districts. Similarly, technology use is integrated into the district's core curriculum across subject areas and grade levels rather than called out as a separate curriculum topic or set of learning outcomes. This approach has advantages in terms of helping teachers see the applicability of technology to the particular subject areas they teach (and we will describe its advantages at greater length in Chapter Eight), but it is hampered in Detroit by the very limited professional development time available. The contract negotiated with the teachers' union calls for only two professional development days per year. Substitutes to cover additional days are difficult to come by in this urban district, and there are limits to what can be achieved through voluntary weekend or summer programs. Detroit schools vary markedly in the inclination of their teachers to devote uncompensated time to their own or others' professional development. The factors associated with teachers' willingness to devote such time were among the issues addressed in our case study research.

Both DPS and CPS participate in a National Science Foundation project, along with the University of Michigan and Northwestern University, aimed at infusing exemplary technology-supported science inquiry curriculum into their schools. In Detroit, efforts related to this Learning Technology for Urban Schools (LeTUS) project have been concentrated at the middle school level. Juanita Clay-Chambers, the Associate Superintendent for Educational Services, explains that the middle schools were seen as the greatest challenge, on the assumptions that at the high school level there were department heads who could help carry the message about the integration of technology with math and science content back to their schools.

Case Study Approach

Within each district, the study team queried district staff, researchers at local universities, and educational technology experts concerning high schools making interesting uses of educational technology. Descriptions of school technology use on the Internet and in national publications dealing with educational technology were consulted as well. In Chicago we made exploratory visits to a number of high schools in addition to conducting telephone interviews with technology coordinators and school principals to help narrow the field of potential sites. A more-limited preliminary appraisal was conducted in Detroit, in keeping with district procedures for reviewing and approving proposals to conduct research in the city's schools.

The schools we selected for study represent a range of educational purposes and characteristics as well as different histories of technology use. Some have long been considered "early adopters" of new technologies within their districts, others are in midcourse or trying to "catch up."

Our Chicago schools comprise a traditionally organized college preparatory school with a mathematics and science focus; a vocational/technical magnet school emphasizing computer technology; and a small, progressive high school stressing student-centered interdisciplinary studies. None of these schools has selective admissions, although the college preparatory high school began a scholars program, admitting 100 students per year on the basis of test scores starting in 1998–99.

In Detroit we conducted fieldwork at a selective college preparatory school, a technology demonstration school, and a general high school located in an economically strapped Empowerment Zone. The broad range of school sizes and missions enabled us to examine technology use in the service of different educational goals.

Once a school was selected as a case study site, we undertook a series of site visits, observations, and interviews over a period of nine months or more. Most of the visits to Chicago schools occurred during school year 1998–99, whereas those to schools in Detroit began in the spring of 1999 and continued through the spring of 2000. Each school was visited by a core team of two researchers with less frequent visits by the study's principal investigator (Means). Interview guides were used to structure initial interviews with principals, technology coordinators, and teachers. These early conversations and associated brief classroom visits provided a basis for selecting two to three particularly interesting uses of technology on which to focus at each school. Subsequent observation sessions were supplemented with opportunistic conversations with students and teachers. Key interviews were transcribed for subsequent analysis. All this information was used in completing a structured debriefing form for each case study school. The school's liaison with the research team was given the opportunity to review the debriefing form and make additions, corrections, or comments.

To provide perspective on the nature of the challenges urban schools face in implementing technology, the study team also visited several suburban high schools in the same regions. Effective implementation of technology is a challenge for any school, and many observers judge that only a minority of U.S. schools in any economic circumstances are meeting this challenge. Nevertheless, urban schools must deal not only with limitations on resources but also with constraints of size, politics, and perceived mission that dwarf the challenges faced in the typical suburban district. Contrasting the experiences of the urban case study schools with those of their suburban counterparts helps to clarify the ramifications of these constraints. By looking carefully at the contexts in which these urban case study schools operate and at the strategies they have used, we can gain a fuller understanding of just what it means for them to try to implement technology-supported "twenty-first-century" learning environments and of the special blend of vision, dedication, and pragmatism it takes to make such environments work.

2

Now We've Come to the Point Where We've Started

MOVING BEYOND PROVIDING TECHNOLOGY ACCESS

The focus on technology at Murray-Wright High School owes much to two young people who never attended school there. Sallie Polk, the school's principal, has a son majoring in computer science in college and a daughter working in the computer industry. Polk credits her children with opening her eyes to the power of technology. When she saw what they were doing with computers, she says, "I immediately said I wanted to bring this world to students at Murray-Wright."

A thirty-nine-year veteran of the Detroit Public Schools (DPS), Polk is skilled in identifying allies and deft in securing funding within the district for her change initiatives. In 1996 the district's Ninth-Grade Restructuring Initiative provided the opportunity to build the first computer lab in the school. The purpose of the lab then was the same as it is today: to function as a center where teachers could bring whole classes for instruction and learning. Polk's desire was to create a technologically literate student body ready for the twenty-first-century workplace, and she felt that improving access to computers was key to meeting that goal. The lab approach was adopted to "maximize support for students and staff in learning the technology," says Polk. She wanted entire classrooms to have access to computers at the same time and hoped that computers would be used to emphasize all "academic strains." She expected, and still expects, that teachers could help students

17

take advantage of what technology can provide them, especially on the cutting edge of what's being used in business.

At first, Murray-Wright teachers had disagreements about access: there was only one computer lab for the entire student body of more than seventeen hundred students. Teachers could not find places in the lab schedule, as slots quickly filled up. Polk soon found funding for additional labs, however, drawing on other sources within DPS and the community. One resource was Detroit's Compact program, a partnership among local businesses, colleges and universities, and the school system to make sure Detroit students meet the academic requirements for higher education. Other external partners have been the University of Michigan, IBM, and the National Science Foundation (through the district's Urban Systemic Initiative grant). By fall of 1999 in addition to the original Technology Center, Murray-Wright had three labs, one each for the math, science, and English departments, and department heads had been supplied with their own computers in their offices.

Polk also has made extensive use of Title I funding to support her technology initiatives, including funding for a teacher to fill the role of technology coordinator at the school. As a school of 1,750 students, of whom 50 percent are on free or reduced-price lunch, Murray-Wright receives extensive compensatory education funds (e.g., over $200,000 in federal Title I and close to $450,000 in Michigan state compensatory education funds in a recent year). The school is located within a federally designated Empowerment Zone and in a neighborhood that has a mixture of empty lots, low-income homes, abandoned dwellings, and recently renovated single-family homes. Although Murray-Wright is a "choice" school, meaning students come from across the city to attend, many students come from the immediate area and from other low-income neighborhoods like the one surrounding the school. Having many students from high-poverty areas has made Murray-Wright eligible for several other programs and partnerships, and Polk has been proactive in ensuring that Murray-Wright finds technology funding to support her vision of greater student access to technology.

Multiple Partnerships with the University and Business Community

Murray-Wright has been actively engaged in a number of school improvement efforts with external partners. Shortly after Sallie Polk identified funds to build the first technology lab at Murray-Wright, she helped develop a partnership with the University of Michigan to build a second lab in the school. The university donated computers to Murray-Wright as part of a three-year program in which university students mentored Murray-Wright students. According to Polk, the university was interested in admitting more qualified minority students into the University of Michigan. They hoped that having Murray-Wright students document their learning in portfolios, with mentoring from university students, would help establish the students' credibility and their ability to perform. The mentoring program was designed to help students develop their writing skills in preparation for completing a pilot version of the ACT that relied on portfolios of student writing. The program paid not only for equipment but also for University of Michigan professors and staff to develop a student-student mentoring program between college and high school students. Students in writing courses at Murray-Wright sent drafts of essays to college students via e-mail, and the college students in turn responded with comments, edits, and suggestions for improving the high school students' writing. The grant also paid for staff professional development in portfolio assessment.

In 1998–99 Murray-Wright became a part of the IBM Reinventing Education: Wired for Learning program in Detroit, a program to enhance parent involvement through building electronic networks between schools and neighborhood housing developments. The program aims to link a cluster of schools and two neighborhood housing developments through teacher professional development and through providing tools for teachers to create Web pages for their classrooms and to post schedules of upcoming classroom and school activities. The Wired for Learning virtual environment includes a Web page designer, threaded discussions, and an on-line conference center where teachers can talk to one another, with students, or with parents. The environment is to be accessed both at school and within two computer labs located within the Jeffries and Park Side housing developments. At the beginning, the environment was accessible only to teachers and staff of DPS, but now any parent can access the environment. One round of parent training has been conducted at both housing sites using the networked learning environment.

To date there are six Detroit schools in the IBM project, each with five to ten teachers participating. At Murray-Wright fifteen teachers have been trained and are registered to use the site. Two of these teachers have created and actively maintained their Web sites with up-to-date lesson plans and calendars. The templates are easy for teachers to use, and recently three Murray-Wright teachers have been trained to act as teachers of their peers in the use of the Wired for Learning environment.

Most recently, Murray-Wright has become a part of Next Day, a national program designed to bring technology and professional development in the use of technology to the nation's poorest communities. The project is to last three and a half years and is administered by teachers and volunteers. At Murray-Wright, participation in the program will be coordinated by Katie Fitzner, the school's technology coordinator. Various local companies will be donating hardware and installation services to bring technology into their classrooms. 3M will be donating cabling for networked computers in all core curriculum classrooms (five to seven computers per room), and Ameritech will be laying the cable and installing networks over the winter break. Training in the use of the equipment took place in the summer and fall of 2000.

These new partnerships have provided many opportunities for Murray-Wright, but they bring new challenges for the school as well. Although the ACT program with the University of Michigan enjoyed modest success from the viewpoint of teachers whom we interviewed, the program ended in 1998, and attempts to establish a similar program with Mary Grove College in Detroit have failed thus far. Talks are unlikely to resume soon and the practice of having college students mentor Murray-Wright students in writing college application essays has not been sustained. The IBM Reinventing Education grant has raised considerable interest among faculty who wish to access the project Web site to begin creating their own Web pages, but the local on-site coordinator has no power to add new teachers to the list of registered users, making expansion of the project difficult.

These are problems that arise naturally when increased access raises the expectation that more teachers and students will be able to participate in technology-supported learning activities. Teachers and students see the promise of new technology, but new institutional relationships and partnerships are often fraught with growing pains and other difficulties. Disappointment is common, and it has been a part of the teachers' experience of many of the relationships that Murray-Wright has formed with industry partners and universities. It's important to note, though, that these partnerships in Murray-Wright's case *were* successful in increasing students' access to technology, as Sallie Polk had hoped. As a result of these partnerships, Murray-Wright is among the richest of all Detroit's high schools in terms of technology resources.

Murray-Wright's Technology Infrastructure

The school's focus on technology is evident after a tour of the various classrooms and facilities within Murray-Wright's campus. The school's 1950s-era building is multicolored, and though the color is still bright, the school grounds show the need for refurbishing and upkeep. The cracked pavement of the tennis court is overgrown with weeds. Inside, the school is a mix of renovated classrooms and older rooms in need of some repair. Many of the newer rooms are the computer labs.

Teachers report that students take extra care in these rooms to ensure that the computer labs have working equipment in them. Katie Fitzner, the technology coordinator, reports that students were initially astonished to see these freshly painted rooms in their school, with clean desks and new carpeting. They have taken care of the room, she believes, because they have a sense of its preciousness within the school environment. Fitzner notes, "The kids would walk by and see this room when it first went up and they would just go 'wow' . . . I mean to see a room like this, carpeted and painted nicely with this equipment in their school, they were amazed. They would come up to me and ask 'what class is this and how do I take it?' I think that when students walk in this room and see how nice it is they act differently."

Chemistry teacher Robert Santavicca reports that when students in his class are not working on computers, they refrain from putting anything down on the long tables that protect the computer screens—they are concerned not to break anything or damage the computers, because they want to be able to use them in their classes.

Altogether there are five major computer labs throughout the school. The Technology Center houses twenty-four Windows machines, all connected to the Internet. There are thirty-six Power-Macs, also connected to the Internet, in the English lab. The lab was paid for through funds from the Michigan ACT project and the Detroit Compact Program. While this English lab was being built the school used state dollars from a school-to-work initiative to build a Business Department lab that houses twenty-four Windows 3.1 machines without Internet access. This lab also was supported by sales from the schools' vending machines. Finally, two math and science labs, each housing twenty-four Windows machines, were funded through the school's participation in the NSF Detroit Urban Systemic Initiative. All of the machines in these labs are designed to have Internet access as well. The Internet connections in the Technology Center and math and English labs are typically all up and running, but the school has experienced a number of problems keeping the science computer lab on-line.

In each of the labs, the computers are networked and enable roughly two-thirds of the average class of thirty to thirty-five students to work individually on a computer. Four of the five labs were installed by an outside vendor with the monitors and keyboards placed beneath desktops and visible via a tinted tabletop. This design allows the classroom teacher to provide instruction in the front of the room without having her or his view of the students obstructed by monitors. Students can look up at the instructor in front of the room or down at the computer monitor beneath their desktops.

The Technology Coordinator: Making Sure It All Happens

A key role in making things run smoothly at Murray-Wright is played by Katie Fitzner, the coordinator of the Technology Center. In addition to staffing this main lab for several periods a day, Fitzner teaches alongside the classroom instructors who sign up for the center. On any given day she may be asked to teach students Web browsing skills, Web page design, or word processing. She may also be asked by a classroom teacher to find specific Web sites to help students conduct research on the Internet. In between teaching classes in the lab, Fitzner writes the school's newsletter, coordinates the school's technology planning team, and is the facilitator for both the IBM Reinventing Education program and the Next Day project at Murray-Wright. Without Fitzner's leadership, Murray-Wright would struggle to keep up with the many partnerships that the school has formed, and teachers with little experience in using technology would have nowhere to turn for on-site advice on how to incorporate technology into their teaching.

Fitzner was formerly a business education teacher at Murray-Wright. When she returned from a maternity leave in 1996, Sallie Polk asked her to head up the new Technology Center and coordinate the school's technology team, consisting of parents, teachers, and students. The team is charged with implementing the school's existing technology plan and modifying it for the future. Fitzner's role is primarily as a teacher leader, but she troubleshoots technology problems with other teachers and provides some technical support as well.

Nearly all the teachers we interviewed mentioned Katie Fitzner as a key resource to them, and she is often busy checking in with teachers in labs throughout the school to find out how things are going. During one school visit, Fitzner was showing us to a room where we'd be observing a class. She stopped to check in with Robert Santavicca, the chemistry teacher who houses the science computer lab in his classroom, about his equipment. They talked for some time, and Fitzner noted the problems he had and promised to look into what could be done and whether they might be able to call on the district for technical support.

For her part, Fitzner has been active in supporting teachers with integrating technology into the curriculum, particularly into long-term research projects that some teachers have been implementing with their students.

Supporting a Project-Based Approach

Some of Murray-Wright's teachers are starting to exploit the school's technology infrastructure for problem- and project-based learning with their students. In the sciences, Robert Santavicca regularly accesses chemistry problems from the Internet for his students to solve, and Julie Oberly has created a project for students to learn about African American scientists. In the foreign languages, where interim department chair Gabriella Gui requires technology to be used in all classes, students have been engaged in creating Web pages about French culture. And in math, students in a new course called "Real World Applications of Math" have used climate data located on the Internet to predict the best week for the school's winter break in terms of saving money on heating costs. The projects that are completed in the Technology Center rely on a partnership between the classroom teachers and Katie Fitzner, whereas teachers like Robert Santavicca in science and Stanley Henry in mathematics, who have their own labs in classrooms, can lead projects on their own.

African American Quilt Project

The African American Scientists Quilt project was developed by teacher Julie Oberly as part of the ninth-grade Integrated Natural Science (INS) class, which serves as a review of middle school science and a preparation for the biology/chemistry/physics sequence. The project involves students working collaboratively in two-person teams to learn about an African American scientist. As part of the project, students develop technology skills that include learning how to conduct Internet research and how to design PowerPoint presentations. The culmination of the project is a fabric quilt that incorporates pictures of each scientist from the students' presentations. The purpose of this project is to make students more aware of the role of African Americans in science and to develop their research and presentation skills using technology as a tool.

The project began with Oberly developing a list of African American scientists. The students then selected which person they wanted to research based on the type of scientist they were interested in studying. Students were asked to find descriptive information about their scientists, including their family origins, educational backgrounds, and early careers. The students worked cooperatively in two-person teams to conduct their research, organize information, and present the facts that they had gathered to the rest of the class. At times, students divided the tasks and worked independently, but all presentations were done jointly.

Students further developed their technology skills by using computers to access the Internet for researching and downloading images, to develop presentations, and to write reports. As part of this project, students also delivered their presentations in front of their peers using PowerPoint software. Each student group designed eight slides and conducted a ten- to fifteen-minute presentation.

Oberly has a list of criteria to evaluate the student presentations. These include dressing up for the presentation, producing complete slides, and answering questions appropriately. The final step in the project involved creating a quilt from the pictures students had found of their scientists. Students scanned the pictures of scientists that the students had collected through their electronic research onto decals, ironed these decals onto fabric squares (in the school colors), and then sewed (with the assistance of parent volunteers) these images of African American scientists together to create a quilt. Students who could not find a picture of their scientist were assigned a letter to depict in an interesting style—these letters spell out "African American Scientists" on the quilt.

At the beginning of each stage of the project, Fitzner provided whole-class instruction on the technology-related activities for that stage. For example, students learned how to connect to the Internet, how to use search engines to look for information about their scientists, how to use PowerPoint, and how to download images and add animation to their presentations. Researchers observed that during some of the project work, the classroom and lab teachers provided support and facilitation as students worked collaboratively on their presentations. However, during a large proportion of the time, especially when new technology skills were being introduced, the two teachers provided direct instruction to the class in a traditional whole-class lecture format.

On the days when SRI researchers observed the project, Julie Oberly and Katie Fitzner team-taught the class. Oberly would support students as they learned about the scientists' roles while Fitzner would teach the specific technology-related skills that students needed to complete the project. For this project, students spent approximately two days a week using the Center's computers throughout the entire semester. The amount of time each week varied depending on which element of the project students were working on at the time. For example, the students spent more time in the Technology Center while they were researching their scientists and less time in the lab when they were downloading the pictures for the quilt.

In discussing the project, Oberly noted that although difficult, the project was successful in promoting her students' motivation and in helping her to overcome the fear of the unexpected in teaching. She describes the stress entailed in trying to integrate technology: "The students get frustrated when they can't find something, they can't do something, and they know they have [only] this hour and I'm helping five other people."

Students, however, must develop independent research skills, and in the end, she said, all the trouble is "worth it." She did offer a few pieces of advice for other teachers embarking on a technology-supported project for the first time. First, she advised teachers to practice using technology on their own first, taking time to learn different applications they might use with students. Second, she suggested it was important to have opportunities to watch other teachers as they integrate technology into instruction. She noted, "After you know what you're doing, it's not scary at all."

The French Culture Web Page Project

The French Web page project is part of the Advanced French class. Approximately fifteen students in grades 10 to 12 participate in the class. The French Culture project, designed to enhance the foreign languages curriculum with a hands-on student-centered activity, helps students learn about French language and culture by giving them the opportunity to gather, analyze, and interpret data; prepare a final product; and revise and edit their work. In addition, through this project, students develop technology skills, including Web-based research and presentation skills. The students work on the project for the entire spring semester.

Gabriella Gui, the teacher for this class and interim chair of the Foreign Languages Department, learned the basics of how to design Web pages through a DPS workshop she and Ms. Fitzner attended. She thought this would be a fun project for students so she purchased Adobe software. Gui would like to further develop the French Web page she has started by using templates provided through the IBM Reinventing Education project. The Reinventing Education Web page templates would support posting quizzes, assignments, and grades. Gui also would like the page to serve as a tool for communicating with parents and keeping them up-to-date about what students are working on.

Before implementing the French Culture project, Gui asked her students what they thought about the project and found that they were very enthusiastic about this activity. According to Gui, they liked it because it was a "break in the routine." They decided as a group what to include on the Web page, and then the students volunteered to research different aspects of French culture. Students worked in groups of two to three on broader topic areas. Within those broad areas, each student selected a particular topic of interest. For example, one group of students researched French music, and a student within the group specialized in French classical music. The students were responsible for researching their topic to gather appropriate information, primarily by downloading images and text from the Internet. Before doing this step, Gui reviewed research ethics. She required students to write for permission to use the images and text. One student in the class volunteered to serve as coordinator of the project to ensure consistency across areas.

After gathering information on their topic from the Internet, students used Adobe software to design a Web page. Katie Fitzner taught the students how to put the information they gathered on their Web pages, which were linked together, to serve as a resource for external audiences. Gui told her students that the whole point is to have visitors to your Web page, and she encouraged students to be creative, to make their pages attractive, and to include the type of information that they would have liked to find. The students presented their information to all the foreign languages students at the end of the semester.

Gui integrated assessment throughout the French Web page project by breaking up the project into small steps and collecting and grading student work at the end of each step. In addition, the student coordinator tracked what students were working on and how they were doing. Among the criteria for grading were conducting research to find accurate information on their topic, analyzing the data, interpreting it, and writing a final product. Gui also graded students for effort but did not assess their design skills per se.

Gui reports that in her experience students who are lower achieving with conventional instruction do better when they use technology. One of the reasons is that there are fewer barriers to completing their work. For example, when she assigns a research project, students have to go to the library and access information. With technology, they go to the lab and all the information they need is at their fingertips. Students using the Internet are less likely to get discouraged by the mechanics of performing an information search, according to Gui.

The Winter Break Blues Project

When researchers visited Murray-Wright in late May, teacher Stanley Henry proudly showed the presentation made by his ninth-grade Math Applications class summarizing their investigation of the choice of week for winter break. Because they are directly affected by the timing of the school break, students were interested in this question. Nevertheless, Henry reported that they hated the project at first because they were unaccustomed to having to figure so much out on their own. As Henry describes his approach, "We guided them out of trouble but let them discover what they had to discover in order to reach a conclusion." Having gone through this extended project with much coaching and guidance but limited direction from Henry, the dozen students in this class ultimately gained a great sense of accomplishment. Henry reported, "By the time they made their presentation, they were celebrating."

Henry gave his students the question about the ideal timing for winter break but did not tell them how to answer it. He did indicate that one criterion for selection of a break week was minimizing the disruption to the academic program, and the class worked through the calendar, rejecting December and January because of other school interruptions in those months. The class focused in on February and the more narrowly defined task of finding the best week for a break during that month.

Once the students realized that savings on heating costs was the second major criterion for deciding when to have the break, they were able to design and carry out an investigation. They wanted to test the hypothesis that the current practice of breaking over the fourth week of February was in fact the best solution given heating costs and weather patterns. They measured their school building to compute its volume (Henry reported that their estimate was "close enough" to the official figure on record), toured the school's boiler room, and interviewed Michigan Consolidated Gas and the school building engineer concerning BTUs and variables affecting heating costs. Henry had initially hoped that they would perform their analysis in terms of BTUs, but the students were not comfortable with the concept and when they argued for analyzing the related and more familiar variable of temperature, he agreed. The students obtained fifty years of temperature data from Detroit City Airport off the Internet. They also found data from Detroit's other airport (Detroit Metro) and considered using that data, but fewer years of data were available for Detroit Metro, and the students reasoned that a longer time series would give them a better estimate.

Henry's students downloaded the weather data into Excel spreadsheets and used the software to obtain the mean, median, mode, high, and low temperatures for each week in February. They created a bar graph showing these means across the fifty years and found that the means for the third and fourth weeks of February were similar and lower than those for the first and second weeks. Next they created a line graph with one line showing the mean temperature for the third week in February for each year and one showing the mean for the fourth week. They found that the line graph gave them a compelling presentation because the line representing the third week in February was pretty consistently above the line for the fourth week across the years. Importing their graphs into PowerPoint, they created a presentation describing their investigation ("The Winter Break Blues") that they presented to a full house on Family Night.

Henry's Math Applications students had access to technology resources as one source of information and to support their analysis and presentation. But the key ingredient here was not the technology per se but rather a teacher who provided a challenging, realistic problem and gave his students responsibility for structuring and working that problem themselves. These students got practice in the statistical concepts of central tendency and in using Internet search tools, spreadsheets, and graphing programs, but more than that, they received practice in designing an investigation to answer a driving question and in using mathematics as a tool for supporting inferences. Over the course of their investigation, they practiced structuring a complex task that involved subproblems, requirements for collaboration, generation of a solution, and a concrete product.

Henry advises teachers who wish to implement similar projects to be guided by a sense of patience and discipline. On the one hand, teachers must be patient and meet students where they are in their problem-solving ability. At the same time, teachers must hold expectations of students and encourage students to develop the discipline to stick to solving problems on their own. Initially, students may not be thrilled about the idea of having to solve problems on their own, but once they realize the teacher is not going to give them the answer, and the answer is to a problem they are interested in solving, they become highly motivated and engaged. Students must have "opportunities to fail," notes Henry, to go down dead ends in their problem solving and start over again, just as they would in solving problems in the workplace. Teachers should provide such opportunities, even as they provide support for developing strategies for overcoming the challenges of any real-world problem like scheduling winter break.

Perceived Impacts of Project-Based Learning at Murray-Wright

Among the gains reported as benefits of these examples of project-based learning were an increased confidence in students' ability to solve problems on their own, increased motivation and student engagement, and greater content learning. Henry notes that students come into his class being accustomed to being told what to do. His projects, by contrast, require students to solve problems on their own. After an initial period of resistance, Henry notes, students gain a sense of independence. Students learn to support their decisions with reasons, and he reinforces an emphasis on argumentation by grading students on how "well reasoned" their arguments were in the class. Students also learn how to "attack a problem," notes Henry. Initially, they would say, "We can't do this," but after delving into the problem, students gained confidence that they could solve a complex problem.

Students in the other two projects benefited as well, demonstrating increased motivation and engagement. One team of two students in Julie Oberly's class said that they liked the African American Scientist project because it was more fun than their regular classroom work. Both girls had computer skills already, but they thought that they had developed additional technology skills through the project. They also reported learning more about scientists both from their own research and from the presentations by other students.

Julie Oberly said that she enjoys developing projects that are "meaningful to students." She added that the project is fun and that it "makes their learning an active learning within parameters." According to her, the benefit of this project is not only that the students have to discover the information about their scientists but also that they have to learn it to be able to present it. She said that she likes the project and will use some variation of it next year because she enjoys "watching and learning from them."

Across projects she has helped teachers implement, Katie Fitzner notes the key role of technology in motivating students: "I've seen so many students who are normally withdrawn and shy about participating in class, but they get on the computers and it just changes—they're excited, they look forward to getting here, they get here quickly to class. It's really nice to see that."

Professional Development: The Big Challenge

Although the projects these three teachers implemented reflect the kinds of projects education reformers have documented as demonstrating how technology can transform teaching and learning, these teachers are but a few of the many teachers at Murray-Wright who would like to integrate technology more thoroughly into their instruction. As one staff member noted, "We are very technology-rich. For the past three years our principal has made acquiring technology her priority. Now we've come to the point where we've started. . . . We've been experimenting with ways to integrate it . . . and we need more. Our old technology plan was more of a technology-buying plan. Now we need to revise it to include staff development and integrating it into the curriculum." Another teacher remarked, "Investing in hardware and software without investing in professional development won't get you anywhere."

Establishing a workable professional development plan—even with the variety of partnerships the school has established—has proven elusive for Murray-Wright for several reasons. These reasons are not peculiar to Murray-Wright; rather they represent conditions in many urban high schools. First, in the past only a few days have been established for professional development in the contract signed by teachers' unions and the Board of Education. Second, teachers' knowledge and comfort level with basic uses of technologies varies greatly. Finally, different approaches to integrating technology reflect widely differing instructional philosophies within the school.

Limitations on Available Professional Development Time

In 1998–99 DPS provided only two days of professional development per year to teachers. In 1999–2000 Detroit's new schools chief David Adamany included more professional development days in his proposed contract to Detroit school teachers. This contract also included a number of provisions related to reduced sick days that became the subject of much dispute. Detroit teachers struck during the first week of school over disagreements about a merit pay plan, and in the deal made to end the strike, professional development days were removed from the contract in return for more sick days.

During the year, substitutes who could fill in to allow teachers to attend staff development activities are hard to come by in this city strapped by severe teacher shortages. Teacher release time for professional development is, as a result, limited at Murray-Wright as it is in many urban schools.

Those training sessions that are offered are either offered during the day, when teachers have difficulty leaving school, or after school or on weekends, with no teacher stipends or incentives for participation. Within the school, some teachers perceive that there is not a lot of support for professional development in technology. Teachers have been instructed to look to the district's offerings for professional development. Attempts to organize the district's Office of Educational Technology staffers to come to present at the school have thus far proved challenging. School staff say that the district office has been slow in responding to the school's requests for training. District staffers, for their part, note that only a handful of people are assigned to work with all of Detroit's schools.

The amount of professional development Detroit teachers receive around technology or any other topic appears to vary widely depending on the extent to which a particular school, or an academic department within the school, has managed to create a climate of collaboration and commitment. Teachers wanting to take advantage of professional development opportunities during the workweek must get other teachers to cover their classes while they are away. This system has worked fairly well in some departments at Murray-Wright. In Foreign Languages, for example, teachers have been able to spend roughly ten days outside the classroom per year. (Only a few of these days are likely to be spent on technology, however.) Teachers in some other departments engage in few professional development activities at all.

Several efforts have been made to integrate technology into the fabric of school life. Katie Fitzner presents at many of the Wednesday departmental meetings, training staff in uses of technology and providing them with information on opportunities to use technology. Fitzner also produces a quarterly newsletter, which highlights technology opportunities in the school. An attempt has been made to provide special technology training for department heads, but its success has been limited.

Wide Variation in Comfort Level and Skill in Using Technology

A number of teachers who were skilled in the use of technology and who integrated it into their teaching noted that many of their peers were afraid to use technology in their classes. Many have never used computers before, and when they do make the first tentative steps toward using computers by signing up for Katie Fitzner's lab, they rely exclusively on Fitzner for teaching the technology components of the projects. Without Fitzner, they would be unlikely to try using technology with their class at all.

Some of the technology-using teachers note that many teachers who have been teaching at the school for a number of years have been reluctant to adopt new technologies. But some new teachers are just as likely to rely on textbooks and worksheets, especially since to date there have not been many computers in instructional classrooms (an issue to be addressed by the Next Day project). Still, many of the eighteen new teachers who came to Murray-Wright in 1999–2000 have signed up to use Fitzner's lab, and they have been eager to integrate technology into their instruction as much as possible.

Variation in Uses of Technology to Support Different Instructional Philosophies

A clear professional development strategy for Murray-Wright would need to consider the wide variations in teaching philosophy among teachers in the school. Some teachers espouse a student-centered or constructivist philosophy, whereas others are firm believers in direct instruction. Supporting each group of teachers, given the limited professional development resources, would be a challenge. And whether or not the use of technology to support more traditional forms of instruction brings enough added value to the learning process would be an important issue for the school's technology plan to consider.

Stanley Henry, whose Math Applications class was described earlier, is among the more constructivist of Murray-Wright's teachers. Technology in Henry's classroom supports students solving problems on their own. Henry shares at least in part a view of mathematics similar to that advocated by the National Council of Teachers of Mathematics. He views mathematics as a language, and he believes students are apprenticed to use this language through exposure and practice. According to Henry: "The reality of learning English, which is a method of communication, is no different than the reality of learning mathematics. It's exposure. If you hear the word 'coefficient' once, it may take on meaning, it may not. But if you hear it five hundred times, you won't even know that you've learned the word, because it's part of you. In reality, mathematics is a tool. That's all it is, just as English is. It's a tool to express something that you have to accomplish."

Our observations of Henry in his Real World Applications of Math class showed how he applies these principles to his teaching. In one class, Henry reviewed the concept of slope with his ninth-grade students, who had recently completed Algebra I. The context of this review is as part of a larger study of weather prediction. In the class, Henry reviewed key terms, including ordered pairs and x- and y-coordinates, before having students enter coordinates into an

Excel spreadsheet. He had the students then graph the points using the charting function of Excel. Students printed out their charts, and Henry had his students form a triangle with a ruler. He then illustrated how slope is equivalent to the ratio formed by the sides adjacent to the right angle that is formed at the meeting of the two axes.

Throughout the lesson, Henry asked his students questions about why they were doing what they were doing. When the students tried to create a formula for the slope, taking the change in y and dividing it by the change in x, Henry asked the students, "What is this for? What is the meaning of this? So we can get the slope of the line?" When students had constructed triangles by drawing lines perpendicular to the y-axis from the higher point on the y-axis, Henry asked the class, "What do we have?"

"A triangle?" ventured one student.

"Yes, but what kind of triangle?"

Several students stirred and searched for the right term. A boy sitting in the back row mumbled the answer, and his classmates repeated his response more loudly. "A right triangle."

"Yes," said Henry. "Now, can you calculate the slope of the line by measuring the y- and x-axes? Remember, slope is vertical run over horizontal run. If you were building a road, you would call it a 'grade.'"

The students look a little perplexed. Mr. Henry asked, "Why would you come up with different numbers than we had before?"

Henry's questions invited the students to think on their own and generate explanations for their answers, much in the way mathematics reformers have advocated as central to developing deeper understanding of the domain. His is a student-centered approach that relies strongly on students' constructing their own knowledge in the course of solving an authentic problem. Henry does not leave his students alone to flounder, however. His questions draw their attention to key details and relationships between new material and things they already know. While the immediate lesson is grounded in content specific to the concepts of slope and y-intercept, the larger context of their graphing is the Winter

Break Blues Project they are working on for the spring, a problem the students are interested in solving. By graphing algebraically in Excel as well as constructing graphs geometrically by hand, students get two vantage points on the concept of slope.

Teacher-Directed Technology Use

Down the hall in the Technology Center, a World Geography teacher is having teams of student pairs research countries, which she has assigned, on the Internet. Students must find the GDP, GNP, religion, governmental structure, and population of their assigned country. In addition, students must find information about technology in their country and about entertainment.

On the board, the teacher has already identified for the students three Web sites with much of the information they will need. One site is like an on-line encyclopedia with geographic information about all the countries of the world, and another is an on-line almanac. The third site is maintained by the U.S. government, and in addition to having basic geographic information on all the countries, has basic military and strategic information (e.g., the length of runways at the largest airports). None of the sites has information about entertainment, so for students to find out about this dimension, they would need to search on their own.

Students in the World Geography class showed different skill levels in searching the Web. As we watched, most were using the three sites identified by their teacher and were copying information directly from the sites onto their pads of notebook paper. Some students searched for information on entertainment on their own (using sites not listed on the board). Many of the students searching for entertainment were perplexed by the many specific sites that came up when they typed the name of their country and the word *entertainment* into the search field. One student toward the end of the class asked the classroom teacher, "What are we going to do for entertainment?" The classroom teacher replied, "If you don't find anything, don't worry about it."

The form of instruction employed in this class reflects a more traditional way of teaching geography. This same assignment might have been given to students with only a textbook or a world almanac at their disposal. To be sure, current up-to-date information may not be available in the school library, and the Internet offers access to better information than the students might otherwise have had access to. But one wonders whether the use of technology adds to students' understanding of geography in this case. Current standards adopted by the National Council for Geographic Education (1994) emphasize geographic problem solving, not the learning of discrete facts, as aids to promoting deeper understanding of the role of space and place in human experience.

It is doubtful that students in this class learned much about browsing or using the Internet for research, either. The one effort students made to find information on their own (searching for information on a country's major forms of entertainment) was not emphasized by the teacher, who encouraged students to move on if they did not find that information. Motivated by the desire to keep students away from offensive Web sites or the pressure to use time in the computer lab efficiently, many teachers are giving students URLs or bookmarks for their Internet search. Although this strategy has its place when learning search skills is not the instructional objective, it does trivialize the search task. Helping this geography teacher and the many others like her learn to use technology effectively as a tool for instruction may require more conversations within the school about learning goals and how technology can support simultaneously deeper investigation of subject matter and the learning of technology skills.

To address these issues, Fitzner has introduced CyberSafari sponsored by Lycos. In CyberSafari, students choose a "channel" or topic and are given instructions to look for information on particular Web sites, which are accumulated as clues that students find as part of a contest. A number of students in the lab resisted using CyberSafari at first, perhaps because they were unused to the open-endedness of the task. Fitzner reports, "One student goes 'This is stupid, this is boring.' She came in yesterday and told me she went on-line at home. Now she comes to me, makes it a point to say, when she has free time during lunch, she tries to come in here and do this."

Other Challenges at Murray-Wright

Several other challenges have faced Murray-Wright since the school began building its many computer labs to increase students' access to technology. Some of these challenges are related only indirectly to technology, but others directly challenge Sallie Polk's vision of ensuring that all students will become a part of the "world of technology."

Student Attendance

Student attendance is a problem at Murray-Wright that a number of teachers in the school cited. According to one teacher, many students routinely arrive fifteen to thirty minutes late to school each day, and first period classes are many times only half-full. Even after the second bell rings to signal the beginning of the next class period, this teacher notes that many students remain in the hallways. Hallway monitors must chase students into class, often unsuccessfully. Other teachers and administrators are frustrated with the problem, and the front page of the school newsletter for Fall 1999 includes a message from Sallie Polk to the school community about attendance policy. Still, the problem persists and, according to some teachers, became worse in the 1999–2000 school year.

Students' irregular attendance has implications for their participation in projects that involve technology. If teachers are signed up to use the Technology Center, and a large number of students miss an introductory lesson on Web browsing or Web page design, it is hard for Katie Fitzner and the classroom teacher to manage instruction so that the rest of the class can make progress on their project while ensuring that students who have missed class do not fall far behind.

Technical Support

As the computers in the labs installed in prior years begin to age (some are already three to four years old, even in the newer labs), significant technical problems have emerged. In the Technology Center, for instance, four computers have not been working since the first day of school. They all need new hard drives before they can become operational again. In Robert Santavicca's lab, none of the computers' Internet connections have been working, so he has not been able to use the Internet to identify chemistry problems for his students. At the time of writing, it was unclear whether the problem was with the network connection to DPSNet, the district's Web server. Not surprisingly, frustrations have run high, as these problems have grown in number and complexity during the past school year.

By and large, teachers tend to rely on their own ingenuity and their colleagues to solve minor technical problems. According to one teacher, "We have a few teachers here who troubleshoot when they can, but nobody has that role, nobody is assigned as a technician. What we have is the vendor who put the Technology Lab in, as well as math and science, and he does everything—the equipment, painting, decorating, everything. Since he's been with our school three years now, he has provided a lot of technical support. Some of that has been free . . . but we now have to pay for it."

Other teachers have expressed frustration with the original lab vendor, noting that it has taken up to a year to order and receive parts for computers. As of 1999–2000 the school had no service contract for support from this or any other vendor; rather, the school began to rely on the district's help desk. The school rates the help desk as generally responsive, solving many problems within a week. The district, however, does not supply parts, and so the four computers with broken hard drives will remain broken until money can be found to replace them.

Access to Computers in the Labs

Most labs in the school have between twenty and twenty-five computers while most classes have between thirty and thirty-five students, so not all students can sit at a workstation when they come to one of the labs. Katie Fitzner believes this deters many teachers from participating, because they want each of their students to be able to have his or her own computer. Sometimes Fitzner splits large classes into two halves.

There is competition for access to the lab, which creates some mixed feelings about the labs, according to Fitzner. As technology coordinator within the school, she has many other duties besides running the lab and coteaching with classroom teachers who use the lab every day. Fitzner often must close the lab while she is away, and some teachers are disappointed that they cannot use the labs as often as they'd like. No one is available to cover for Fitzner, which means that the lab is not accessible during all periods of the day. Fitzner is investigating upgrading and adding new computers to the main lab, since the Technology Center is used by the whole school. The technology coordinating committee would also like to find space to house additional computers that could be used as a place for students to drop in to write papers using word processing software.

The School's Plans

One of the most promising developments of the past year has been the school's successful application to be a part of the expansion of the Ford Academy of Manufacturing Science (FAMS) program. The program promises to bring real-world, challenging content to students, as well as more technology to the school in the form of seven to ten networked computers and participation in a distance learning program sponsored by Wayne State University.

The school was one of three in the area competing for the program, which aims to help students prepare for the workplaces of the twenty-first century. Students start the program in tenth grade and must meet some basic application requirements to participate. (At Murray-Wright they must have a 2.0 GPA or greater, have passed algebra and one science course, and must live in the Empowerment Zone.)

Six teachers are teaching in the FAMS program: two math teachers, two business teachers, one English teacher, and one science teacher. Although each will teach his or her own section of the course, they plan to meet regularly to discuss the program and to ensure that it is meeting its goals. Each teacher will take a turn coordinating the project. The teacher who is teaching the current section will be responsible for maintaining contact with the district's FAMS representatives and keeping the other teachers informed of what's going on in the program. Among the more interesting student projects proposed are designing a business, creating Web pages, and building a model home. For the home project, students will have to use knowledge of physics principles and geometry to build a scale-model home out of wood planks.

Perhaps the most promising aspects of the FAMS project are the opportunities for teacher collaboration afforded by the program. Many of the teachers with whom we spoke and whose projects we observed were isolated from one another, meeting only when the technology team met to conduct strategic planning and address ongoing technical support problems. The FAMS program meetings provide a different opportunity for teachers to share successful strategies for integrating technology into project-based instruction and to build models of collaborative teaching that other teachers in the school could emulate. The FAMS teachers all have a common planning period to support their program.

More recently the school has become a part of the Atlas Communities school reform program conducted by the Education Development Center (EDC). A part of this program involves having the school form study groups of no more than six teachers each on issues of concern to the school. This program will provide an opportunity to build greater teacher collaboration and collegiality within the school. Experience at other schools suggests that an increase in the extent of teacher collaboration would have, as a by-product, positive impacts on the effort to infuse technology into instruction.

Support for projects like the FAMS program and the Atlas Communities program at Murray-Wright is critical if Sallie Polk's vision of bringing access to the world of technology—the real world of work, that is, in which technology is used to solve complex, ill-defined problems—to all students at the school.

3

Toss the Typewriters!

CONNECTING TO THE
NEW WORLD OF WORK

Originally a general high school, Bogan Computer Technical High School became a computer magnet school in 1988 under Chicago's court-ordered desegregation plan. Like many of the former magnet schools, Bogan is now a combination general high school and "options" school. Roughly half of Bogan's students come from its immediate neighborhood on the far south side of Chicago. The other half are selected through a lottery from a citywide pool of applicants seeking inclusion in the computer technology options program. Each year, some three thousand students from across the city of Chicago apply for the 150 openings in the technology program.

Technology plays a central role at Bogan, which was cited by *Family PC* magazine as one of the nation's "top 100 wired schools" in 2001. As the school describes itself in its technology plan, "Using modern computer technologies, we prepare students for the modern world of work and life-long skills using modern technologies for survival."

Located in a working-class neighborhood with an ethnically diverse population, the two-story school building is forty years old but well maintained and in the midst of a major renovation. It has gotten new windows, floors, ceilings, and a new science laboratory, along with major renovation of its swimming pool and modifications for handicap access. Students give a casual air to the school uniform of white tops and black pants. Bogan's 1,847 students (as of September 1997) are 46 percent African American, 26 percent Hispanic, 21 percent Caucasian, and 7 percent Asian. Just 4 percent are limited in English proficiency; 76 percent qualify for free or reduced-price lunch. Incoming students fall in the middle of the range of test scores for the district.

Innovative Programs and Activities

There are quite a few programs and activities at Bogan with features associated with education reform (Lee, Smith, & Croninger, 1995). Bogan has ten periods a day with staggered starts; each student attends for eight of the periods. Core courses for ninth, tenth, and eleventh graders meet every other day for two periods. The longer class periods support more complex activities, including the use of technology.

A related innovation at Bogan is the use of interdisciplinary thematic units. In October 1998, for example, staff met to develop instruction around the theme of conflict resolution, a topic selected by the principal. In the spring of 1999 the school implemented a second all-school thematic unit on diversity.

Four years ago Bogan was among the first ten schools in Chicago to join the Chicago Systemic Initiative, a program to revamp and improve science and mathematics education districtwide, funded by the National Science Foundation. Participation has brought staff development funds to Bogan, which the principal has used to support Bogan teachers' attendance at technology conferences (e.g., sending twelve teachers to the National Educational Computing Conference) and visits to other schools making extensive use of technology.

Bogan is one of thirteen high schools in Chicago implementing the pre-International Baccalaureate (IB) program. Each year thirty students from Bogan's regional attendance area who have strong academic records and high test scores are selected for this demanding pre-university course of study. Bogan has applied for IB accreditation, and once accreditation is received, students will be able to take the IB exam and receive college credit for IB courses completed at Bogan.

Twin Thrusts for Technology Use

There are two complementary thrusts to Bogan's use of technology. First, the school seeks to give students technology skills that will make them highly employable, whether or not they go on to college (45 percent do). In keeping with this emphasis, the school seeks staff and programs that will keep their offerings up-to-date, featuring the software and other technology areas that are strong in the marketplace. Principal Linda Pierzchalski explains: "With our technology classes, what we are trying to do is work with business and see what does business want with a kid when they graduate from high school, and these are the kinds of software packages we are teaching them [students]."

Second, the school views technology as a support for learning any content area. This second thrust is much closer to the role Von Steuben (see Chapter Four) envisions for technology. So in addition to offering courses in the latest software applications, computer programming, and so on, the school encourages incorporation of technology into its English, mathematics, foreign language, and other courses. Technology advantages cited in the school plan include the ability to individualize a learning program, access to information on a just-in-time basis, the ability to connect to broader communities outside the school, and extending the time available for the "engaged learning" promoted by the Illinois State Board of Education (ISBE).

Bogan's Technology Infrastructure

Bogan has more than three hundred PCs, all 486s or above and capable of running contemporary software, connected to the Internet through the school's local area network (LAN). The school has

one T-1 line funded by a state technology grant and a second connected to the Chicago Public Schools (CPS), funded by the district.
About two-thirds of the school's PCs are located in one of eight
computer labs, each containing twenty to thirty computers. One of
the labs is designated as a student drop-in lab, which students may
access before and after school and during lunch. When the lab is in
use by classes during the day, students may be given permission to
work independently in the lab if space is available. There is also a
computer resource room (or "playroom" as the principal calls it) for
teacher use. At a minimum, each classroom has a computer for
teacher use as well as a VCR, television monitor, and converter that
permit projecting the image on the teacher's computer monitor
onto a large screen. There are also forty-some laptop computers for
teacher use and a videoconferencing facility.

In keeping with its role as an option school for computer education, Bogan has an ambitious technology plan. The plan calls for
providing five to six computers for every classroom. By spring of
1999 over a third of Bogan's classrooms had attained this level of
equipment. In the process of installing these connections, the
school became aware of the need for major upgrades to its electrical
system and LAN. Oracle is consulting on the school's network and
has recommended an upgrade from its current 10 MB to 100 MB.

This much technology requires a sizable human infrastructure
to keep it running and help teachers take advantage of its capabilities. Bogan has two full-time staff members largely devoted to
technology administration and technical assistance. Owen
McAleenan, the school's technology coordinator, has been at
Bogan for over thirty years. A former math and computer technology teacher, McAleenan wrote the original proposal for Bogan to
become a computer magnet school. McAleenan chairs the school's
technology committee responsible for framing its technology plan,
trains teachers, maintains equipment, helps with student scheduling and attendance, and helps prepare the school budget. Mike
Matyasec, a former math teacher, serves as network administrator,

operating the school's LAN. Salaries for both McAleenan and Matyasec come from desegregation funds. McAleenan's position is justified on the basis of his role in handling scheduling and keeping classes racially balanced. Matyasec's position is seen as essential to providing the educational activities appropriate to Bogan's role as a technology magnet school. In addition, whenever the school writes a proposal for grant funds, it incorporates a request for funds for equipment maintenance, which can be used for part-time employees.

In addition to these two full-time staff members, two college students (funded with Perkins money) work part-time on technical support. Bogan's TRN consultant from the district visits the school on a weekly basis and keeps them apprised of district activities and potential opportunities to receive support from CPS. The school does not look to the TRN for teacher training, however, feeling that its own staff is too advanced to profit from the level of training district TRNs are offering.

Bringing an Entrepreneurial Spirit to School Technology Implementation

Bogan staff are unanimous in citing principal Linda Pierzchalski as the driving force behind technology at the school. Pierzchalski became Bogan's principal in 1994, after serving for four years as assistant principal. Pierzchalski fills three interrelated roles with respect to technology use. First, she is active in setting the vision for technology's role. She keeps in touch with networks of technology-using schools and with curriculum and school reform movements generally. After forming ideas about how she would like to see technology use enhanced, Pierzchalski then fills a second vital role in developing strategies for promoting these uses among her faculty. A combination of incentives, opportunities, and requirements is used to influence teacher behavior. At the same time, Pierzchalski is active in acquiring resources to support the use of technology at

Bogan. The acquisition of these resources makes it possible for Pierzchalski to offer her staff incentives in the form of professional development opportunities and equipment. Participation in funded programs at the same time expands the vision of technology use of Pierzchalski and her staff.

Making Deals

With a sly smile and a twinkle in her eye, Pierzchalski describes the deals she has negotiated with the district Department of Learning Technologies, business partners, and her own staff. She clearly is always on the lookout for opportunities, enjoys negotiations, and brings a daunting supply of energy to making arrangements work to Bogan's advantage.

Pierzchalski has a strong relationship with the district Department of Learning Technologies and is tuned in to opportunities there. She often volunteers to participate in pilot technology programs and usually manages to obtain some equipment or other advantage in the process. When the Department of Learning Technologies wanted to start a pilot program to use laptop computers in classrooms, for example, Pierzchalski volunteered Bogan as a pilot site and then argued successfully for leaving a dozen of the computers at the school after the pilot was completed.

Another example is Pierzchalski's teacher laptop program. Believing that greater access to technology for their own use would encourage her (non–computer education) teachers to make greater use of technology in their teaching, Pierzchalski started a program to offer teachers laptops for classroom and home use. Teachers had to write a brief proposal describing how they would use the computers and agree to spend seventy hours of their time getting technology training or training others to use technology. About forty teachers wanted the computers and submitted a proposal. The hours the successful candidates "owed" Pierzchalski in exchange made it possible for Bogan to offer both computer education courses after school for parents and an extensive array of before-school technology classes for teacher colleagues. Pierzchalski points out that if you compute the value of the time the teachers are contributing in dollars, it in fact exceeds the purchase price of the laptops, and everyone comes out ahead.

Pierzchalski has also been alert to opportunities for funding from outside organizations. Sharing a ride back to Chicago from a Springfield ISBE training session with several Chicago elementary school principals, Pierzchalski and her car-mates decided that their schools would meet the ISBE's definition of the kind of "nontraditional wider community" the state wanted to fund. The resulting proposal did indeed garner a Technology Literacy Challenge Fund grant. Pierzchalski advises: "Write a lot of grants and do a lot of proposal writing because no matter how much you get from federal or the district, there are always more needs."

Bogan has been a participant in three Technology Literacy Challenge Fund grants from the state of Illinois. Pierzchalski says their initial plan provided a base for a second and third proposal and that this vision is the best explanation for why Bogan has received three of these grants. One of these grants paid for Bogan's first T-1 line and its Web server. Bogan has also received a grant from the Annenberg Foundation to do staff development on the use of technology with two elementary schools.

After company representatives did a stint at Bogan as "principal for a day," both Oracle and Acxiom were impressed enough with Bogan to want to make a contribution. Acxiom, a data storage and integration software company, has provided students with opportunities to do job shadowing, and the company has donated $25,000 for purchase of software to support diagnosis of reading difficulties. Oracle has provided technical consulting on the upgrading of the school's LAN and is donating fifty computers. Oracle is also planning to start a database administrator program at Bogan (to be described later).

With assistance from McAleenan and other staff, Pierzchalski has brokered all of these deals, without which Bogan could not mount a technology program at the level it now enjoys.

Influencing Teachers

Moore (1991) brought a marketing perspective to characterizing the population's proclivity to adopt new technologies. If you think of a bell-shaped normal curve, at one end you have the tail of the curve, about 3 percent, who can be characterized as "innovators." These are people who seek out new technologies and always want to be on the cutting edge. A little after them, there is a somewhat larger group, perhaps 15 percent of the population, whom Moore calls "early adopters." These individuals may do less to seek out the newest and the slickest, but once a technology's utility is demonstrated, they will embrace it. The trick, Moore tells technology developers, is to move beyond the innovators and early adopters, to lure the great bulge of the bell curve—the "early majority" and the "late majority"—to use your technology.

The same principle applies to teachers. Outside the computer education department—where technology use is mandatory—teachers will need differing degrees of support and encouragement to make technology use part of their practice. Teachers at Bogan have no doubt that Pierzchalski would like to see them incorporate technology into their teaching. She has used a variety of strategies to increase their comfort with new technologies and to influence their use of them.

One step has been the requirement that teachers use a computer-based system for reporting attendance and submitting lesson plans. Pierzchalski chose these tasks because they are familiar teacher functions that are easy to do with technology. In conjunction with the requirement for electronic submission of attendance, she made sure that each classroom had the needed teacher workstation and offered in-house training on how to use the software. Hence, the mandate to use computers for administrative functions came along with the needed equipment and training. Many of the teachers who were not computer users prior to Pierzchalski's mandate to use them for attendance and lesson planning have subsequently chosen to use software for keeping track of grades and for word processing.

Another strategy that McAleenan cites as effective is the designation of a core technology team for each subject area. These teams support others in their subject area in implementing technology use by providing training on how to use software technology and on technology troubleshooting and by serving as a resource for ways to integrate technology into instruction. Bogan has technology teams for the core subject areas—English, math, science, and social studies—and a foreign language team is planned.

In school year 1998–99 nineteen different Bogan teachers offered forty-five training sessions for their colleagues. Topics ranged from Basic Computers: How Do I Turn This Thing On? to using particular pieces of software (Grade Quick, Lesson Plan Express, and Excel) to Internet resources and teaching strategies (e.g., classroom management and block scheduling use strategies). Initial on-site teacher training sessions focused on the use of technology per se, but over time, teaching issues involved in technology use have received more emphasis.

In addition to the laptop computer program, Pierzchalski also had a teacher computer resource laboratory set up to offer teachers a chance to play with new technologies in an informal, unstructured setting. She encourages teachers to attend conferences and take training in technology use, finding funds to support their professional development. When teachers need additional resources to support technology use in their classrooms, they know that if they go to Pierzchalski with a good rationale for why the desired resource will support student learning, she usually will approve the purchase. As English teacher Trent Eaton, one of the heaviest technology users outside computer education, says, "It's very rare that I've been told 'no'."

One of the factors contributing to staff retention at Bogan is the knowledge that Pierzchalski is skilled at obtaining resources for the school and supportive in using these resources to promote teacher innovation and learning. Both McAleenan and Matyasec have been recruited by the district office (McAleenan even completed the training to become a TRN consultant) but have declined to leave Bogan. Pierzchalski views providing her technology staff with ample professional development opportunities as a necessary investment toward keeping them at the school.

Pierzchalski tries to involve her teachers in the kinds of activities she would like to see them implement in their classrooms. One of Pierzchalski's plans is to have teachers form study groups to do research on trends in curriculum within their respective academic disciplines. "Study groups are going to be a big thing next year. . . . I have been making the recommendations up to now about different forms of engaged learning, but I want them [the teachers] to do some research and actually train with each other, and you know, do some reading and be able to present to the faculty and say, 'Based on our research, this is what we have seen happening, and you know, this seems like this might be a good way for us to go.'"

Pierzchalski envisions these groups as modeling lifelong learning for Bogan's students. In the same vein, she would like for teachers to start doing more portfolio assessment in their classrooms. In 1998–99 she required her teachers to submit portfolios of their work: ". . . kids learn from modeling, and if you model something, kids will model it too. So I said if I made teachers do a portfolio and they saw the value of it, then there is a chance that some of them, not all of them, will try some sort of variation of the portfolio next year, which is an alternative for those kids who cannot handle a regular paper-and-pencil test but are very creative."

Advice from an Activist Principal

Based on her experience fostering technology use at Bogan, Pierzchalski has several nuggets of advice for other school administrators.

Set an example yourself. Pierzchalski believes that principals need to know more about technology themselves and to model using technology for personal productivity: "I think the principal has to be behind it [technology]. And the principal has to model for the teachers and show the teachers that she uses it or he uses it. That they see it as a valuable tool."

Pierzchalski would like to see the CPS invest in increasing principals' knowledge of educational uses of technology. It is difficult for principals to exert pressure on their faculties to use technology if the principals do not do so themselves. Moreover, given the organizational structure of a district like Chicago, where decisions concerning technology and expenditures for it are made at the school level, a principal who is a technophobe is likely either to opt out of technology use altogether or to be at the mercy of whatever vendors market the school most aggressively: "The first thing is that none of this [technology implementation] is going to go anywhere until the district trains the principals. Because the principals don't know what they don't know. And there are so many of them that I have seen that are really afraid to even turn on a computer . . . we have e-mail on the computer, and they don't even pull up their own e-mail. So until you get the principal on-line, no matter what you do systemwide to train teachers, it is not going to go anywhere. . . ."

Do not rely on technology standards to set the content for teaching technology. Several states and national organizations have recently disseminated standards for technology competency (see, for example, International Society for Technology in Education [ISTE], 1998). There has been some discussion of the possibility that CPS might adopt technology standards in the form of a required curriculum for a ninth- or tenth-grade technology course. Although Bogan already provides a required technology course to freshmen and Pierzchalski thinks this would be a good practice districtwide, she does not believe that adoption of formal technology learning standards would be effective: "The way the system operates, and it takes so long to write the standards, I would be against them [CPS] writing standards because by the time they wrote the standards, we would be past those software packages and into something else."

Start with something easy. Pierzchalski recommends requiring teachers to do something with technology but making sure that the requirement is well within their level of capability. At Bogan, keeping attendance, grading, and electronic submission of lesson plans were used in this way. Pierzchalski did not expect everyone to begin incorporating technology into their teaching at once, but rather looked for signs of progress:

> Everybody in this building can do their lesson plans and do their attendance [electronically], and they are proficient at it. I would say even looking at their portfolios, you can see that more and more of them have made the attempt at using computers in the classroom, whether it is for word processing and doing their tests . . . they have learned that it is easier to do a test on the computer. A lot of them have adopted now the Grade Quick program. . . . I am beginning to see sheets of paper appear with all of the students' names and their total points to date, what assignments they have turned in. I have seen at report card pickup . . . more in April than in November . . . if your parent came in and you weren't doing well, here's the grade sheet for you, here's exactly what your child did. Or even at a [parent-teacher] conference, say, "Let me go to the computer" . . . . [Teachers] can go to the computer and pick up the grades.

Be flexible and give teachers room to experiment. Pierzchalski does not view technology skills as something you can simply mandate or "give" to teachers. She recognizes the need for teachers to have time and exposure to multiple models of technology use, so that they can form their own ideas about how technology fits into their curriculum and practice: "You have to be flexible enough to know that they [teachers] need to have time . . . so that they can go and see what is new and see how they can adapt it. . . . "

Recognizing that as teachers go through this process of technology adaptation and adoption they will have their own ideas about how to use it, Pierzchalski recommends giving teachers a lot of latitude and support: "And they [principals] have to be open to ideas that the teachers may have regarding it [technology], to let them be creative. I think it comes to a certain point in time too that you have to develop a relationship with your faculty where they are not afraid to try new things, and if it doesn't work, it doesn't work, we go back to the drawing board."

Arrange for teachers to learn technology use from their peers. The primary mechanism for teacher learning about technology implementation at Bogan is on-site sessions offered by the school's own "high-end" teacher-users. Pierzchalski believes that time needs to be set aside for staff development on technology use, regardless of other demands on that time. At Bogan, 60–75 percent of on-site staff development time is technology related.

Pierzchalski emphasizes teachers' preference for learning from peers operating in settings similar to their own. When the CPS held its first citywide technology fair in October 1998, Pierzchalski arranged for three buses to take all of Bogan's teachers to the fair. She saw this cost as a bargain. She would like to see the district offer more training geared at higher-level technology users, with groups of teachers having similar approaches to technology use coming together to share approaches: "It would be really nice to bring those really good [teachers] who use a lot of multimedia together and just to have some kind of open forum to talk about what they have done or to show, you know, a five-minute clip of 'what I have done' kind of thing. Because that is how they learn best—from each other."

Pierzchalski warns that you cannot simply take a model that works well in suburban school systems and assume that you can transfer it wholesale to an urban classroom. Rightly or wrongly, urban teachers see the two contexts as so different that successful strategies for the suburbs are not relevant to urban practice.

> And one of the big things that the teachers would have a real fit about . . . is do not bring someone in from the suburbs on how they do it [use technology]. Bring someone from within. Because the attitude of the teachers when you bring someone in from the suburbs is like . . . "they pay the teachers X amount of money and they do this, this, and this. Well, that is never

going to happen in Chicago." So, you know, bringing a model of "this is what I want you to do," but not supporting it with the same level of financial support turns teachers off. So don't bring me the suburban district that has one of these rooms where you could just automatically send a little note that says I want *Gone With the Wind* shown today at 9 o'clock, and at 9 o'clock *Gone With the Wind* appears on the screen. It needs to be in-house people who are really doing the things that [they] are training. In-house people because there is nothing that turns off Chicago public school teachers [more] than bringing a suburban person in.

Confront the diehards with drastic action. Even harder than getting the large central portion of the population in Moore's technology adoption curve to take on a technology innovation is converting the far-right end of the curve—the "laggards" with strong resistance to changing their tools even if a new technology is easily available and clearly superior to old methods. Pierzchalski asserts that a principal needs to be willing to confront the diehards with drastic action in order to convince them that they cannot continue doing things in the old way: "You know, if you have a classroom with typewriters, that teacher is never going to teach keyboarding on a computer with the typewriter sitting there. So you've got to have the guts to take the whole classroom of typewriters out and toss them."

Be creative in identifying and leveraging resources. Because most of the costs of technology implementation—the human support structure as well as hardware and software—have to be borne by individual schools under Chicago's decentralized organizational structure, the principal needs to be zealous and flexible in locating and allocating resources. One of Pierzchalski's greatest strengths is her ability to identify resources and figure out how to use the resources she has to generate more resources for the school. A set of laptop computers, for example, turned into a mechanism not only for getting teachers more familiar with technology but also for getting them to plan ahead their use of technology (in their proposals to receive laptops), and to participate in training others including community parents.

Teaching Technology Skills

All Bogan students are required to take a basic computer course as freshmen. This course provides an introduction to spreadsheet, database management, word processing, graphics, and communications applications as well as keyboarding skills. A second computer course, selected from eleven different courses in the computer education department, is also required for graduation. Those students who are in the computer technology option program take four computer education courses. Offerings during the 1998–99 school year included desktop publishing, computer applications, programming (BASIC, PASCAL, C, COBOL), Internet use, data processing, and an Advanced Placement (AP) computer science class.

A Workplace Approach to Computer Applications Class

Marilyn Foster, who teaches the Computer Applications class to twenty-one sophomores, used to work in industry as a legal secretary. She received her teacher certification through Chicago State University, where she received her degree in Business Education (with an endorsement in Computer Science), after deciding on a midcareer transfer from private industry to the Chicago schools.

The Computer Applications class uses a book designed for industry (*Learning Microsoft Office 97* by DDC Publishing) rather than a text designed for the school market. Foster counsels: "My advice to urban high school teachers using technology is to keep the focus on skills that students will need to further their education or get a job."

Foster tries to bring the expectations of the world of work into her class. Care in following directions receives emphasis in her assessments and grading. The practice of students checking their own work before submitting it is a class norm. Following workplace practice,

Foster does not look at draft products; once a student submits a piece of work, it is assessed for his or her grade. Students know they need to check their work thoroughly before submitting it. They are encouraged to enlist the help of their peers when they have questions and to get peer feedback and suggestions before submitting work to Foster.

Foster incorporates the content that the computer technology department has specified for this course but is free to sequence the units and to vary the time spent on them as she sees fit. At the beginning of the course, she gave students a survey concerning their knowledge of computer applications and has used the results of the survey in planning her course. Upon finding that few students had spent enough time on PowerPoint in their freshman computer applications course to feel confident using that application, for example, Foster decided to give it more emphasis with her sophomore students.

For each application, Foster has students read assigned sections of the text, complete exercises, and then create a product using the relevant application. At the end of the PowerPoint unit, for instance, each student gave a three- to five-minute PowerPoint presentation, using the TV monitor to project their work for the whole class. Typically Foster provides a set of issues or current events from which students choose their presentation topics, but she leaves content details up to students. During the whole-school thematic unit on "conflict," for example, she had her students do Internet research on the Microsoft antitrust trial and present arguments either for or against the government's case.

Foster tries to stress general communication skills in this class in several ways. She instructs her students to be prepared to explain the concepts they read about to the whole class in addition to having them present the products of their work to their classmates. She has contacted the English department to find out the skills students are learning there so that whenever feasible, she can stress the same skills in her Computer Applications class.

The advice Foster offers to other teachers on how to teach technology skills shows that she does not try to be the all-knowing expert with her students but instead encourages an expectation that technology learning is a lifelong process: "Admit that you don't know everything there is to know about the technology being used. Tell them that the person responsible for creating it doesn't either. Remind them how new and how dynamic technology is and encourage them to use the 'help' feature. Have students help other students. Designate peer tutors and give certificates. And, by all means, ask the advanced students how to perform some procedure even if you already know how."

Mixing Technology with Love and Marriage

To fulfill the CPS requirement that students acquire research and writing skills, all Bogan freshmen are enrolled in a Process Writing class. Students taking Process Writing from English Department chair Elizabeth Wagner in the spring of 1999 were also taking either regular freshman English from Trent Eaton or honors English from Steve Biegel. Eaton's students had just finished reading *Shabanu*, a romance set in India. Biegel's class had just completed a unit on *Romeo and Juliet*. During February the three English teachers jointly implemented a thematic unit on love and marriage customs around the world as a follow-up to these readings.

Wagner sees benefit in such joint projects not only in terms of integrating the curriculum for students but also in terms of giving teachers a chance to learn from each other's varying styles, strengths, and weaknesses. Wagner had met with the other two English teachers at the beginning of the year to explore options for integrating the curriculum across their courses. The Love and Marriage unit fit not only the two reading selections but also with interest in the topic natural to their students' developmental stage and to the occurrence of Valentine's Day in February.

For the Love and Marriage project, students were assigned to four-person groups, each of which selected a religious or ethnic group to study, performed research on the chosen culture's courtship and marriage customs, prepared a multimedia presentation, and gave their presentation to the class.

Each group member took on one of four roles: researcher, writer, presenter, or producer. The producer acted as project manager, with final authority to make decisions and responsibility for getting the project completed. Producers assigned grades to the other three members of their group. The teachers then graded the producer on the basis both of the quality of the group's product and the appropriateness of the grades the producer had assigned to teammates. The grades counted for both Process Writing and English.

After selecting the religious or cultural group they wanted to study, each student group performed their research on the Internet and in the library. Microsoft Word and PowerPoint were used in preparing presentations. Visual aspects of the various presentations included pictures downloaded from the Internet for inclusion in PowerPoint slides, posters made from Internet pictures using a special copier in the library, and (live) costumed reenactments of ceremonies.

Presentations were videotaped and graded by all three teachers. The principal contributed a pizza party as a prize for the class earning the highest grades. The videotaped presentations were shown to parents on the evening they came to Bogan to pick up their sons' and daughters' report cards.

This unit was the first time these freshman students had been expected to combine Internet research, computer use, and group work all in one extended activity. As we observed Eaton's class of twenty-one students, he began with homework announcements, a brief quiz, and a review of the steps in the Love and Marriage project. Students were expected to complete their research during the (Monday) class being observed so that they could rehearse their presentations on Wednesday and present for videotaping on Friday. After these announcements, students went to work either singly or in their groups. A number of groups continued their Internet research on one of the five computers in the classroom. Several students went to print out pictures downloaded from the Internet. One student searched the Internet for "Islam" and then narrowed the results by adding the word *marriage*. A group doing

the Hindu marriage ceremony fretted about how to make appropriate costumes for themselves. They hit on the idea of using Bar-
bie dolls instead to minimize the difficulty of producing costumes.
Another group opted to go to the library to perform their research
because no more Internet-connected computers were available in
the classroom. (Two of the classroom computers have problems
making network connections that Eaton has been unable to fix.)
Upon getting to the library, the students found the computers
there occupied as well. Eaton circulated through the classroom to
see what work the students had completed and to answer questions. He was also frequently asked to solve technology problems
("Okay, I've now got three printers working.")

In Elizabeth Wagner's Process Writing class, the students we
observed were continuing their writing for their Love and Marriage reports, using either Word or PowerPoint on one of the
classroom desktop computers or one of a half dozen or so laptops
Wagner distributed at the start of class. One student went to one
of the Internet-connected computers against one wall of the classroom to continue Internet research. Wagner too had to cope with
several technical problems (two of the laptops were not functioning). She periodically called for attention from the entire class to
remind students of something she noticed some students needing
help with (e.g., how to start the PowerPoint slide show).

Wagner views technology as a tool for increasing students'
interest in their academic work, "Anytime you've got a toy, you've
got the student hooked." Eaton shares this philosophy and uses
technology strategically. He typically introduces Internet usage to
his students just before Christmas break to maintain their attention
in the face of the impending holidays. Similarly, as the school year
draws to a close, he brings a digital camera into his classroom and
lets students incorporate digitized photographs into their reports
and presentations.

Wagner notes several advantages of using technology with students. Her students take pride in producing products that look just
the way they want them to and are eager to fix mistakes to achieve

the desired level of quality. They also cooperate well while using technology. Students doing Internet research for the Love and Marriage project, for example, derived great satisfaction from finding sources for other students' topics as well as for their own. Wagner also cites a desirable side effect of such multimedia projects in that they can be presented to parents. Parents other than the students' own are likely to see each student's work, and as a result of seeing student work, parents not only feel added pride in the school but sometimes get interested in taking the evening computer classes Bogan offers. Some parents have also decided to buy home computers for their children after seeing displays of student work.

Parent Involvement with Technology at Bogan

Bogan's administration has not always had smooth relations with the local school council, but there has been agreement about the importance of students learning technology. ("This is one thing they don't argue about," comments the school's technology coordinator.)

A community survey conducted in 1996 found that 75 percent of survey respondents felt they needed training in current computer technologies. Bogan started offering evening computer classes for parents and the local community in school year 1997–98. The school had more than three hundred sign-ups that year and nearly as many in 1998–99. Researchers observed evening computer classes on the Internet and on the Windows 95 operating system. Some twenty to twenty-five parents, all from the school neighborhood, attended each session. Their past experience with computers ranged from no prior experience to computer owners who wanted to improve their efficiency in using their home resources. Bogan's technology coordinator comments on this effort's success in creating a new bridge between parents and the school: "We had a pretty good turnout last night. . . . The parents are pretty good, and they're kind of fun. . . . I think they like to come up here when they're not told to come up here 'cause their child has done something wrong."

Bogan has planned expansion of its Internet Web site to facilitate communication with parents. Parents and students will be able to send e-mail to teachers and to get the monthly school calendar, parent newsletter, school newspaper, and course descriptions on line. In November 1999, updates to the site were on hold until the system upgrades could be completed, possibly by the end of 1999.

Planned Corporate Partnerships

Bogan is negotiating with three major technology providers—Oracle, Novell, and Cisco—for new vocationally oriented training programs. These companies are providing equipment and training to selected high schools to help generate a greater pool of qualified potential employees. Each of these programs would be three years in length, to comply with a new Illinois state requirement for all vocational education programs. The Oracle program would train students to be Oracle database administrators. The Novell program would qualify students as certified network administrators (CNAs). Discussions are also under way with Cisco to bring the Cisco Academy, which trains students to install and maintain network systems, to Bogan. The skills these programs would develop are highly marketable in today's economy where companies that use Oracle, Novell, and Cisco products are in great need of staff to use, troubleshoot, and maintain them.

The Novell program is being pioneered at Bogan and has yet to receive state and board approval. The program cannot be implemented until the state obtains additional information on the program's standards and goals and how it fits into the state vocational education program. When this approval is obtained, Bogan will implement the program. Because the Cisco Academy has already been approved by the state, Bogan has proceeded with this program. In November 1999 two staff members received training for their Cisco network certification so that they could begin teaching the three-course sequence on networking technology.

Bogan is interested also in developing partnerships with local businesses to give students the opportunity to work on real-world tasks and give businesses and students exposure to each other. As part of an ongoing effort to revamp and expand its desktop publishing course to create a three-year program, Bogan plans to start an after-school student enterprise program with $10,000 of funding from CPS. Students will bid to do projects, such as business cards, menus, and advertising, for local businesses. The service will be advertised on the Bogan Web page, where businesses will be able to contact the students and request bids. In November 1999 the program received district approval for a 1999–2000 school year start.

Technology Implementation Barriers and Strategies

At the time of our case studies, Bogan had made the most progress among case study schools in wiring regular classrooms. Even so, completion of the infrastructure described in its technology plan was going to require something on the order of $200,000 to $500,000, by the principal's estimate, to upgrade the electrical system and the school LAN to make classroom access (for five or six computers per room) a reality. Through a capital improvement program from CPS, Bogan did improve electrical capacity to classrooms, reaching seven outlets per classroom. It also used E-rate funds to buy diffuser boxes for additional electrical power upgrades.

Bogan does a great deal to stretch the funds available for technology. Corporate partners have donated consulting and equipment. The school has been actively involved in obtaining grant funds to support technology use and has received equipment and training from the district in exchange for serving as a test bed for new programs and equipment configurations. Bogan has been more successful than most urban high schools in obtaining resources for technology use—in part because technology is central to its mission and in part because of the active role the principal has played in this regard.

Scooping up funds from so many different sources has a potential downside, however. Each grant, corporate partner, or district experiment has its own purpose and needs. Each requires staff time and effort to implement. At times, staff may feel they are on a "roller coaster ride" with rushes of momentum for one program after another. Schools need to attain a livable balance. Lack of external collaborations or new programs often leads to stagnation, complacency, and boredom among staff. On the other hand, it is easy to lose focus and program coherence, as well as to burn out some of the most dedicated staff, when too many special programs are going on at once.

Spreading innovative, appropriate use of new technologies to larger portions of the teaching staff is always a challenge, even within a school devoted to computer technology; teacher after teacher cited lack of time to learn new technologies. Bogan is addressing this problem by devoting significant portions of teachers' paid flex time to technology training, offered right at the school before or after classes. The teachers' contract provides for eighteen minutes of flex time a day, or seventy hours a year. Pierzchalski cut a deal with her teachers to devote twenty-four to twenty-five hours of their flex time to in-service training. This arrangement has in effect stretched the time available for professional development, and roughly 60 percent of the in-service hours are devoted to technology. In 1998–99, for example, Bogan teachers had the option of receiving training on Excel and Lesson Plan Express before or after school. Thus, technology training is provided at a time and place that is convenient for most teachers.

There is a downside to this approach for the more experienced, high-end technology users. They find increasing portions of their time eaten up by training and assisting others. They are also called on to serve on committees related to technology, further reducing the time they have available to learn new software or plan technology-supported projects for their own classes. Technology classes offered on-site and by the district are typically too elementary to meet their needs. Other supports, such as equipment for their classrooms and opportunities to attend conferences or visit other technology-using schools, are used to support their professional growth.

The emerging partnerships with business are expected to provide further training opportunities for high-end users among Bogan staff.

Even with the school's technology emphasis and all the training resources and incentives for technology use, some Bogan teachers reportedly remain uncomfortable with technology. In some cases, teacher turnover, through retirement and self-selection, may be more likely than buy-in regarding technology use. When Bogan lost three teachers to a new magnet school, for example, Pierzchalski commented that she was not disappointed, since they had been very traditional in their instructional approaches. She shares the experience of Von Steuben's Rich Gazda that new teachers coming out of education schools are not necessarily better prepared to incorporate technology into their teaching.

Although Bogan has more technical support staff than most high schools in Chicago and all interviewees praised their competence, there is not enough staff to support the amount of equipment and network connections at Bogan. Teachers say they use their support requests "wisely" and cannot call on the technical support staff "for every little thing." They report that a problem with a teacher's workstation will be fixed by the end of the day because it is critical for tracking attendance as well as supporting instruction. A major problem, such as an entire classroom going off-line, will typically be fixed in a day or two. Other problems can take up to a month to get fixed, and this lag discourages technology use by novices who cannot deal with equipment malfunctions themselves. Teacher Trent Eaton encourages teachers starting to use technology to do contingency planning: "Back-up plans! Constantly—especially when you're starting out. You're never going to know what's going to work."

Bogan teachers implementing classroom projects supported by technology, such as the Love and Marriage unit described earlier, have found that most of their classrooms are not large enough to really support this kind of small-group work with technology components. Teacher Elizabeth Wagner explains: "If I had my wish, it would be an enlarged room. . . . Technology needs space. . . . You have to be able to send one group away from another group, and there has to be significant distance. Otherwise, they can't concentrate on the task. You can have all the technology in the world, but if the kids are on top of each other, nothing gets done."

Bogan maintains good relations with CPS, but there are nevertheless disadvantages to being part of a large, urban district. Large districts tend to have more layers of bureaucracy, and such layers typically make for slow decision making. The speed of technological change and the staid pace of district decision processes are way out of sync. This mismatch is apparent when, for example, the district tries to set policy concerning technology purchases: "They [CPS] have tried to come out with standards for what kind of computers we buy, and by the time they come out with the standards, that is the old model. It is obsolete, and they can't move that fast because, you know, by the time you get all of the signatures. . . ."

Although many schools report reluctance to devote time to technology-enhanced projects because of the press of state- or district-mandated content standards and assessments, Bogan does not appear to feel this pinch. The CPS does not have content standards for the computer technology classes, giving them free rein at least for now. In core courses for which the district does have content standards, teachers at Bogan, like those at Von Steuben, think of technology as a tool for getting students interested in a dry topic. As English teacher Trent Eaton says: "When they [CPS] mandate certain things—especially if I think they're terrible—that's when technology plays a bigger part to get them [students] interested in whatever it is."

On average, Bogan attracts a student body with test scores close to CPS district averages. Their test scores are high enough that the school is not in danger of takeover, and staff do not appear to feel unduly pressured by the statewide testing. Principal Linda Pierzchalski would like to see her teachers think of technology as a tool for improving student learning of the content measured in the statewide exams ("That's something we're constantly working on"). One technology-reluctant teacher commented that if the statewide exams mandated that students use technology, such as graphing calculators, teachers such as himself would be encouraged to use it in their teaching.

Plans for Expanded Technology Access

At the end of school year 1998–99, Bogan was well on the way toward expanding the level of technology access provided to teachers and students. Bogan had been approved for an E-rate grant of $36,000 to purchase a server to upgrade the capacity and speed of the school's network. In addition to 50 computers being donated by Oracle, the school was in the process of purchasing 140 new computers, using a three-year low-interest loan from the district that will be repaid from Bogan's allocation of state Chapter I funds.

Bogan plans to place the new computers in computer labs, with the computers currently in the labs being distributed to classrooms to fulfill the goal of five computers in each regular class. In keeping with her usual approach of getting something for something, Pierzchalski will have teachers write proposals to get the computers in their classrooms. The proposals will explain how the teacher plans to use the technology with his or her students, and Pierzchalski is encouraging uses ranging from project-based learning to skills remediation.

The new computers will also support the creation of two new computer labs, one for English and one for mathematics. Bogan is purchasing two software programs, Algebra Assistant and Calculus Assistant (both by Mathpert), for the new math lab. Described as "intelligent educational software," these programs offer a practice environment for solving algebra and calculus problems with options for hints, assistance, or step-by-step solutions. (Technology coordinator McAleenan hopes to add Geometry SketchPad as well.) The technology coordinator hopes that these programs will stimulate Bogan's math teacher to try out some nontraditional instructional strategies.

The reading lab will have a program, purchased with $25,000 from Acxiom, for diagnosing reading problems through tracking and analysis of eye movements. Another new system coming to Bogan is the EduCart (by Acer). The EduCart is an integrated, mobile cart containing a PC, Tegrity camera and software, an LCD projector, and a document camera. Using the cart, teachers can use applications such as Word or PowerPoint to prepare class lessons that can be projected to a whole class using the LCD, broadcast live on the Web, or recorded for later Web access. Notes, microscope slides, and 3-D objects can be incorporated into the presentations. Acer will provide initial teacher training, and McAleenan expects Bogan's science teachers to be participants.

McAleenan and Pierzchalski find that teachers like computer labs because they make it possible for every student to have his or her own computer and for all students to be working on the same task at once. For non-technology-using teachers, movement to teaching in a computer lab, where all students are doing the same thing, is less challenging than movement to the kind of multigroup, project-based work occurring in the Love and Marriage project described previously. McAleenan and Pierzchalski hope that once teachers become comfortable using technology within the computer labs, they will have an increased appetite (and comfort level) for technology use within their own classrooms.

With their upgraded network, Bogan plans to offer teachers home access to the school's intranet and free Internet access from home. After a year of piloting this program with twenty teachers, the school expects to be able to offer comparable access to students. To the extent that teachers use the EduCart to prepare lessons and post them on the Web, students would be able to view lessons from home.

Summary: The Principal's Pivotal Role

Although Bogan has some creative, innovative technology users among its teaching staff, the prime mover for its program is clearly principal Linda Pierzchalski. She has exerted leadership in articulating the purposes for using technology at Bogan and has designed and implemented a multifaceted effort to create incentives and support technology use. A consummate deal maker, Pierzchalski uncovers opportunities for funding and staff development. She finds ways to make arrangements with external funding agencies, the district, business partners, and her faculty where both sides win. When their efforts bring exciting technology-supported teaching and learning to Bogan classrooms, the students are the ultimate winners.

Leaving Bogan, the visitor wonders what technology use there would look like without Pierzchalski's leadership. Does an urban high school have to have a principal willing and able to put this much energy into supporting technology use to make such changes happen?

4

Don't Call Us
a Computer School!

TECHNOLOGY IN SUPPORT
OF ACADEMICS

Some parents of prospective students are reportedly put off by Von Steuben Metropolitan Science Center's location east of Cicero Avenue, but in April 1999 it was evident that this Chicago school receives good care. Gardeners had just put fresh mulch around the trees in front of the 1929 school building, and the grass was newly cut. The stretch of Carmen Avenue on the north side of Von Steuben had brand new asphalt. Not coincidentally, the prime minister of Britain and mayor of Chicago would be visiting the school the next day.

When Prime Minister Blair expressed interest in visiting a Chicago public school in connection with his visit to the city, his staff remembered two students from Von Steuben who had participated in a Young People's Summit (held in conjunction with the G8 Conference) with the prime minister in 1998. With just a few weeks' notice, arrangements for the visit were made, and the high school was ready to put its best foot forward.

Two students who had done an outstanding PowerPoint presentation for their science fair entry were recruited to work with students in a history class to research Blair's life and create a welcoming multimedia presentation. On the morning before Blair's visit, the resulting CD-ROM played continuously on a laptop computer placed in the glass-fronted display case in the school's front hallway. Newly installed miniature speakers played the sound track as digitized photographs and text described Blair's transition from long-haired Beatles-era band member to Labor Party leader and prime minister.

At the end of the hall loomed an enormous digitized photograph of Blair's face, consisting of hundreds of tiny squares colored by students in an art class according to a computer-generated key. Up close the image was an indecipherable melange of individual squares. At the end of the hallway, Blair's visage was easily recognizable.

In the freshly painted Writing Center with its thirty-six computers, a small group of girls worked after school to produce a book on famous Chicago women for presentation to the prime minister's wife and to Mrs. Daley.

Von Steuben is one of Chicago's many options high schools, drawing students from all over the city. Von Steuben has 1,397 students in grades 9 through 12 and shares its aging building with a middle school. The high school offers a college preparatory program with a mathematics and science focus. As one student wag put it, "We're a ghetto, but we're intellectual."

A lower proportion of Von Steuben students come from low-income homes than is typical in Chicago Public Schools (CPS). However, with something over 60 percent of them eligible for free or reduced-price lunch, the student body would hardly be judged as economically privileged on a national scale. Except for one hundred students accepted annually on the basis of test scores for its Scholars Program, the student body at Von Steuben is selected by lottery with preference for current students' siblings and ethnic composition roughly comparable to that of the district as a whole.

Von Steuben students have the third highest test scores in the district, trailing only two schools with test-based selective admissions. At 94 percent daily attendance, Von Steuben has one of the best attendance rates in the CPS. Its dropout rate of 4 percent is well below the district average of 16 percent. Even more impressive, 92 percent of Von Steuben graduates go on to postsecondary education.

Vision of Technology Use

Von Steuben has a clear sense of its mission and the role technology can play in supporting that mission. The school seeks to prepare a diverse student body for college admissions, with particularly strong preparation in mathematics and science. Students are required to complete three years of mathematics and three years of laboratory science as well as one year of computer science to graduate. Technology is viewed not as an end in itself but rather as a tool for enhancing learning in the academic content areas and an inevitable part of doing mathematics, science, and all kinds of other professional and learning activities in the years ahead.

The school's view toward technology's role in its mission was clearly illustrated recently when the CPS used a different name for the school in a draft of materials designed to help parents choose schools for their children. When it was announced that the school might undergo a name change and be called Von Steuben Computer Technical School, Principal Gazda immediately contacted his local school council. Staff and council were united in their opposition to a name change that would give the impression that Von Steuben is a vocational school and leave out the mathematics and science focus that sets the school apart. Although the school is strongly committed to enhancing its use of technology, it views technology as a means of enhancing learning in other areas rather than an end in itself. The first goal in the school's 1999–2000 school improvement plan, for example, was "improving the instructional program through greater use of technology and improved curriculum."

The vision of an expanded role for technology and strategy for its introduction were introduced by Gazda's predecessor as principal, Harold Keihm. Keihm recruited Gazda, who has a degree from the Illinois Institute of Technology and had been involved in developing technology learning goals for the CPS, to come to Von Steuben to help support the introduction of technology. Keihm and Gazda's strategy for introducing technology was to develop support structures for teacher learning and collaboration with recognition and incentives for technology incorporation.

One of the earliest expressions of this strategy was the provision of classes for teachers on how to use spreadsheets for keeping track of grades and attendance. Von Steuben's administrators believed that helping teachers see technology as a support for their own productivity would increase teacher comfort levels and their willingness to experiment with instructional uses of computers.

A second prong in this strategy was the development of a Writing Center. Rather than following the more common strategy of developing an all-purpose computer lab with a technology-oriented lab director to maintain the computers and network, Von Steuben invited English teacher Lucja Kowalski (now the English Department chair) to develop a computer-based center for teaching writing. Kowalski was initially unenthusiastic about having responsibility for computers, but she was interested in promoting the process-based approach to teaching writing that she had studied through the Illinois Writing Project and summer course work at Dartmouth: "Then the opportunity came when this room was available on the fourth floor, and the department chair said, 'Lucy, would you like to look into this?' And I said, 'I don't want to deal with computers. I like the idea of what computers can do, but I really want to work with students. I don't want to sit with machines.' I was a little afraid of it. And then I investigated it, and I said, 'I'll try it.'"

Kowalski began by inviting other English teachers to send her their students who were having difficulty with writing. With several dozen computers and some round tables for small-group work, Kowalski got students involved in peer editing as well as working one-on-one with her: "Little by little. I started just with the English Department. Meeting with them. 'What assignments do you have? No, no, don't change your assignments. Let's just talk about it.'"

Thus, Kowalski started with her colleagues' own instructional goals, and collaborated with them on strategies for meeting those goals. Technology happened to be a support for those strategies, but was not "pushed" on teachers as an end in itself: "It wasn't just [that]

I was introducing technology, but 'Let's now approach writing—even without the computers—[in a new way].' I had kids switch after they'd do some writing, switch partners to another computer to look at that [writing] and have some questions for them to answer based on what they were reading of their partner."

Kowalski then began a quiet campaign of working with other English teachers one by one to get them interested in a process approach to writing as practiced in the Writing Center: "It was incredible to me how much an agent for change that Writing Center became. The teachers who used to just lecture. I'd get them. I'd talk [them] into coming. I didn't try to convert everybody. I started with one or two. Then others go, 'Wait a minute. You did this with that person. What do you think?' Then other teachers who were real traditional, real classic . . . I said, 'Can I take ten minutes of the class and try something?' And then they'd go, 'Oh, this peer editing isn't so bad. . . .'"

Kowalski is careful to respect the goals and content expertise of the teachers bringing their classes to the Writing Center, but at the same time, her own experience as an English teacher allows her to work with students on writing skills rather than technology use only. When a teacher first signs up for the Writing Center, Kowalski discusses general procedures with him or her; for example, the need to have students bring their own diskettes. She gets a copy of the assignment the students will be working on and makes suggestions concerning the incorporation of technology. In general, the regular classroom teacher acts as the primary content expert when his or her students are in the Writing Center. Kowalski is sometimes asked to be the primary expert in certain areas, however, such as reference citation style: "I cater to the individual teacher and design each lesson or approach to what the teacher wants. The teacher comes to me and says, 'I want to do this and this' and you know, I'll ask, 'Do you want me to support writing style and software use questions?' Some teachers will say, 'Would you please talk to them about this and this for ten minutes?' Some want to do it themselves."

In general, Kowalski and the regular classroom teacher are able to act as a team, effectively lowering the student:teacher ratio and making more individualized attention feasible. "So when the students would come in, the two of us would go around and work individually with the students. Work on polishing, answering questions. The teacher would usually give me a handout that he or she had given them so I knew exactly what the focus was, what the teacher was looking for. I always meet with the teacher beforehand. 'Where are the problems? What do you want me to zero in on? What have you told them to do or not do?'"

Gradually, teacher users of the Writing Center have expanded beyond the English Department and also beyond traditional writing and editing to include preparation of multimedia presentations. "Last year one of the senior teachers was having her students . . . do research. And after they did the research paper . . . she came to me and said, 'You know what? I would like them to present their ideas to the class but not read the paper. Not go over the whole thing, just key points. Can we do something? You know, a presentation, a visual?' We worked out a slide show . . . I got them to scan in some visuals. . . . Some students actually brought videotapes and we did a video clip in the slide also."

Kowalski keeps track of Writing Center usage. In 1997–98, for example, 381 class periods were scheduled in the lab. About three-fourths of these were English classes with the remainder coming from other departments. Individual students can also come to the lab before or after school or during their lunch period to work on assignments. Writing Center hours are 7–7:30 A.M. Monday through Friday, during class with a pass, during lunch periods, and 3–5 P.M. after school Monday through Thursday. This availability is particularly important for students who do not have computer access at home. In 1997–98 Kowalski recorded 6,497 individual student visits to the Writing Center, double the usage rate in 1991–92, the center's first year of operation. In 1998–99 the number rose to 9,412.

Interactions in the Writing Center

A popular activity within the Writing Center over the last several years has been the development of books of student poetry and other writing. In addition to the usual desktop publishing of text and scanned artwork and photographs, Kowalski has invested in equipment to create hard covers for the student books, and every year they have gotten more professional looking. Jayshree McKechnie, a first-year English teacher, was impressed by the books created by Von Steuben students in previous years and decided to have her freshman English students create poetry books as a way of thoroughly learning the poetry forms and conventions that would be tested on the district's Chicago Academics Standards Exam (CASE) examination.

McKechnie provided considerable structure for the assignment. Students were directed to write ten original poems, including one haiku and one sonnet. They also were required to select five published poems by someone else and to produce "reflections" on both the published poems and on five of the poems they had written themselves. Six class periods in the Writing Center were scheduled for the project. Sessions in the Writing Center were interspersed with time in the classroom, where students continued to talk about poetry concepts and to edit their draft book material. Intermediate deadlines for submitting drafts to their teachers and peer editing helped keep students on track during the course of this three- to four-week project.

Kowalski created a template for students to use in creating the books after prior experience suggested that students sometimes have difficulty with a two-page layout. The template simplifies the production process, allowing students to concentrate on content rather than the mechanics of production.

On the day of our observation, Kowalski started the class off by giving an overview of the technical steps in book production. She cautioned students to save their work both on their diskettes and on the computer hard drive so that a backup would be available if a problem occurred. She used a projection monitor to show students how to access and use the template she had created. She demonstrated how within the template they could choose any fonts, effects, graphics, or images they liked. Kowalski asked which students had a computer at home and expected to use it on this project; she took these students aside to show them a translation program that would enable them to move work back and forth from home to school.

During the rest of the class, Kowalski functioned as both technology and content coach. Students asked her questions about how to save their documents, how to use the template, and how to change fonts. Kowalski encouraged the students to enter their poems first and then worry about effects and fonts. She advised students to refrain from using clip art because of its canned appearance.

McKechnie also roamed the Writing Center responding to student questions. She too got questions about how to save documents, use the template, and change fonts. McKechnie was able to answer her students' queries about the technology.

At one point, McKechnie spotted a student staring at his computer screen in frustration. She went over to him and began talking quietly. The student told McKechnie that he did not want to enter his poems because they were not good enough. McKechnie sat down next to him and engaged him in a conversation to draw out his specific concerns. They focused on a poem about a demon, and McKechnie helped the student articulate what he would like to make better about the poem. With this coaching, the student was able to pinpoint the source of his dissatisfaction—his description of the demon was just not as scary as it should be. McKechnie continued to work with the student, discussing techniques to increase the impression of danger.

Almost all students were intent on their task, most working from paper printouts of the poems they had previously written and stored on diskette. The students generally appeared comfortable working with the word processing program (Word). Most of them quickly made changes in format, and they responded to the color underlining Word uses to denote likely spelling and grammar errors. Some of the students knew how to use the scanner and began independently working on picture files. Students sometimes leaned over to ask each other questions, either about a feature of Word, about spelling, or about the content of their books ("What should my title be?").

In talking to the researchers, students in this class expressed interest in being able to create a professional-looking finished book. They had clear ideas about how they wanted their pages to look and were willing to spend extra time to achieve the desired effects. In addition to covering the poetry terminology that was part of the district curriculum, these students would have a memento of freshman English in which they could take great pride.

Creating Creatures in the Writing Center

In May 1998 teacher Carmen Gonzalez gave her freshman biology students an assignment to "Create a Creature" with characteristics and a habitat that go together, given what they have learned about ecology. After researching the features of their real or imagined chosen creature in the library and on the Internet, students prepared a HyperStudio presentation describing the creature and the ways in which it is suited to its habitat. Gonzalez viewed this long-term project as a way to maintain students' interest as they reviewed ecology concepts that would be covered on the district-mandated CASE for her course. Her grading criteria required students to describe their creature's habitat, method of getting energy, food web, special behavior, and any special interactions with other organisms (such as parasitism, commensalism, or mutualism). Students spent ten class periods in the Writing Center working on this project plus whatever time they chose to devote to it outside of regularly scheduled class. Gonzalez gave students the option of working on the assignment in pairs, in part because there were not enough computers for the entire class but also to gain experience in collaboration.

As we observed students working on the Creature project in the Writing Center, they were in the middle of their HyperStudio work. They appeared to need little direction in using the software. As Kowalski toured the center, she examined one student's slide and suggested that the background color made the text difficult to read because of low contrast. The student searched for an alternative color as Kowalski moved on to examine the work of two girls doing a presentation on lions. She suggested that their points would be clearer if presented as bullets. When the girls asked her how to make bullets in HyperStudio, Kowalski realized that she did not know herself. She interrupted the class to ask whether any of the students knew. Finding that no one knew the procedure, Kowalski promised the girls that she would find out.

Kowalski talked to other pairs, reminding them to use a research format and give proper citations to information and graphics pulled down from the Internet (a strong concern among teachers at Von Steuben). Gonzalez moved through the lab, too, responding to student questions and prompting students to incorporate terms and concepts from the class into their presentations.

> Student: I have a question about . . . for getting energy, you put like this food description. . . .
>
> Gonzalez: Well, you know that. . . . Is it carrying out fermentation? Is it carrying out photosynthesis? Respiration? [pauses for response] Method of getting energy.

Gonzalez reports that her students enjoyed the project and that creating multimedia presentations that they will show to their classmates gives a major boost to the level of pride students take in their work.

Our observation was made during the second year that Gonzalez implemented the Creature project with her freshman biology students. Before starting the project the first time, Gonzalez, who describes herself as a novice technology user, went to Kowalski with an outline of her plan, and the two collaborated on the procedures that would be used. Even with the careful planning, the Creature project did not go smoothly the first year. That year Gonzalez's students were new to HyperStudio and had to spend more time just mastering the software. Their problems were complicated by the fact that different computers in the Writing Center had different versions of HyperStudio; if students changed computers from day to day, some of their earlier work sometimes got lost or garbled. They also experienced problems with the server being down on multiple occasions.

After completion of the Creature project the first year, Gonzalez sat down with Kowalski to discuss the project and how it could be streamlined. Knowing the project and its needs, Kowalski and other Von Steuben staff were better able to support it the second year. For example, when students worked in the Media Center during the research phase of the project, the center's director pointed them toward scientific Web sites he had identified in advance where they could locate appropriate images for their presentations. Another facilitator in the second year of implementation was the fact that Gonzalez's students had already had experience with HyperStudio in their required freshman-year computer class. In addition, all Writing Center computers had the same version of the program, and the server was up and running the entire time. Finally, Gonzalez had gained confidence in her ability to design and direct this kind of technology-supported long-term project. Nevertheless, it is unlikely that she could have done so, or would have undertaken the risk of doing so, without the advice and support from her Von Steuben colleagues.

From Library to Media Center

Like many high schools, Von Steuben has moved from a predominantly print-based library model to a media center featuring electronic resources. Many media centers, however, continue to think of their functions as those of a library—supporting the location of information resources. Often the Internet-connected computers in such centers are tightly monitored by the center director and make only a limited contribution to instruction in the core curriculum. Von Steuben's Media Center is a combination library and computer laboratory, and like the Writing Center, it is unusually well integrated with regular classroom activities.

Randy Snow, the center's director, brought a vision of integrating technology, research, and curriculum to Von Steuben's Media Center. Aided by a full-time assistant in keeping the Media Center equipment running, Snow works with classroom teachers to schedule and support their use of the center's twenty-nine computers. The room itself is large with light wooden paneling and shelves of books around the perimeter. The center of the room is filled with tables. Half of the room supports use of print materials and video-conferencing. On the other side of a curtain, tables hold the computers and two printers. An adjoining room contains a scanner and photocopier.

Snow believes that the Media Center should support the instruction that goes on in regular classes.

> I think there's an attitude here— even [among] teachers who don't know a lot about technology or how to implement it in the classroom—teachers feel comfortable coming to the Media Center and asking questions. Some I can't answer. But just asking questions [is useful]. How to use technology? How to fit it into my curriculum? Usually I can come up with ideas of what I can do. I try to encourage teachers to at least take a chance to see what might happen. The one thing I have done is make sure teachers know that I'm here as a resource to them. I consider the Media Center to be an extension of the classroom, and the one thing I do is try to talk to teachers and see what's going on in classes and to offer ideas on how the Media Center might help.

Regular classroom teachers confirm their comfort in consulting both Snow and Kowalski concerning uses of technology with their curriculum. Teachers who would not feel comfortable trying technology-supported activities entirely on their own know they can count on these colleagues as resources. The fact that the principal has been able to piece together funding for the nonteaching center-director positions is important. As a biology teacher told us, it is easier to collaborate with Kowalski and Snow than with other teachers because they do not have regular classes. Not only do they have greater flexibility in scheduling their time, clearly part of their job is to collaborate with other teachers.

Teachers schedule use of the Media Center, typically bringing their class after a topic and task have been started in the classroom. When students arrive at the center, they are expected to start working immediately. Students can seek help from Snow, their teacher, or a peer, if they encounter difficulties. The teacher and Snow also watch out for students who are not progressing so that they can offer direction before a student gets too far behind.

Snow had four years of experience teaching English at the community college level before coming to Von Steuben. He describes himself as "not a techie" and insists "I want to make sure kids know I am a research guy." He is eager to support the content aspects of work done in the Media Center, for example, by working with an English teacher to codesign a Web site to support her classes' study of *The Pearl* or by creating an annotated list of appropriate Web sites for use in another class's research on McCarthyism and *The Crucible*.

Snow credits his principal with the leadership role in identifying and promoting a place for technology within the school. "I have the most supportive principal you can imagine. [One] who, number one, understands the importance of technology, and the importance of technology for research purposes too. He doesn't just see it as having computers and the Internet. He sees [that] it's important to subscribe and pay for . . . the research databases, which are expensive."

Gazda has promoted Snow's continuing education ("He knows that it's important that I know how to use these resources"), for example, by encouraging Snow to take database and PageMaker classes offered by CPS.

Gods and Goddesses in the Media Center

Kerry Catlin, an English teacher in her fourth week at Von Steuben, decided to introduce her freshman students to Internet research as part of their unit on mythology. Catlin was motivated to try using Internet research with this content because she has found that students usually have a low level of interest in mythology. She has found also that when freshman students are assigned to do a written report, they are likely to go to the encyclopedia and simply paraphrase the entry found there. Her hope was that by involving her students in conducting Internet research and creating multimedia presentations, she would increase their interest level and get them to "tell a story" based on what they had learned rather than spitting back what someone else had written.

Before her class took their scheduled turn in the Media Center, Catlin met with Snow to discuss her goals for the lesson. Students were to select a god or goddess from Greek mythology and find information and visual material on them on the Internet for use in preparing a five- to ten-minute presentation. During their meeting, Snow asked Catlin about her own familiarity with Internet research and learned that she felt comfortable with her skills in this area.

After meeting with Catlin, Snow got on the Internet himself and compiled a list of relevant URLs, which he gave to Catlin that same day. When the class came into the Media Center, they had these URLs available to them as well as the guiding questions that Catlin wanted answered in each presentation (e.g., how the god or goddess was created). During the class's session in the Media Center, Catlin herself fielded the majority of student questions. Students sought her assistance when they had trouble finding enough information on their chosen mythological figure. Catlin directed students not only to other Web sites but also to books in the library. Questions directed to Snow during this session tended to be more technical: How do I make this picture bigger? Which printer is this computer connected to? How do I save material from this Web site onto my diskette?

In talking to a researcher after the class session, Catlin noted that the Media Center brings out different behavior in some students. She was particularly impressed by one of her students who typically got involved in conflicts with other students in the classroom. In contrast, in the Media Center he proved to be particularly adept at locating information resources and after completing his own research turned to helping several classmates with theirs.

Students' Media Center Activities

CPS provides Von Steuben with subscriptions to *Britannica* and *Information Source* databases. The school subscribes to additional research databases paid for from its discretionary funds. Although the databases are expensive, Snow feels they are essential to doing serious research. A number of Von Steuben teachers have expressed concern about the mixed quality of sites on the Web, and Snow believes the databases go a long way in addressing this problem.

Snow notes that as Von Steuben students and teachers have become more comfortable with Internet research, teachers use the Media Center more efficiently. Units that once would have required three class periods in the Media Center because of the number of technology issues that would have to be dealt with during the research session can now be completed in a single session. English teachers are the most frequent users of the Media Center, perhaps because of Snow's own English background and his attendance at English Department meetings where he can make suggestions and drum up interest.

Like the Writing Center, the Media Center is also available for use by individual students after school (until 5:00) and during students' free periods. During the 1998–99 school year the Media Center was used by 1,800 individual students per month. On the day when Snow was interviewed after school, for example, sixty students were using the center even though there was to be no school the next day. Snow notes that many of the students who come to the center to use the computer and Internet resources do not have computers at home. Those who do have computers at home come less often and for briefer periods, typically to check their e-mail.

Snow started an after-school technology club in 1998–99. Club members come into the center during lunch and at other times to act as student mentors helping other students with their hardware and software needs. They also volunteer time to help Snow keep the computers up and running.

Snow has been teaching himself Web page design and plans to teach these skills to the club members and then have them create an external Web page for Von Steuben. (Snow himself created the school's internal Web page.) Snow hopes to have his students enter the ThinkQuest Web design contest.

Snow also is considering working with his student technology mentors to offer miniworkshops for their fellow students during the forty-five-minute advisory period on topics such as getting an e-mail account and copying and inserting graphics into documents.

Technology Use in Teaching Science

Of the noncomputer departments at Von Steuben, the Science Department is second only to English in the extent to which teachers are incorporating technology into their instruction. As one would expect given Von Steuben's history and mission, science teaching is very strong at Von Steuben. The two-foot grand trophy for the city's hotly competed science fair is prominently displayed in the school's front office. Three science teachers—two in physics and one in biology—illustrate the department's use of technology.

Technology Use in Physics Classes

Mary Jo Arnashus and Nancy Schlack teach separate physics classes but do much of their planning together. A shared lunch period enables them to codesign units that cover the district-required curriculum standards for regular, honors, and AP physics.

They began trying to incorporate technology into their work five years ago when a district-mandated move to fifty-minute classes eliminated Von Steuben's ability to combine two forty-minute class periods to provide for eighty-minute science labs. Their hope was that the science labs could be conducted more quickly with technology supports since students could, for example, work with computer-based simulations instead of always having to set up equipment themselves or could get the computer software to generate graphs from their data rather than having to plot each point by hand. Arnashus and Schlack say that they taught each other how to use technology such as Science Workshop, Interactive Physics, and the Pasco sensor equipment.

Arnashus and Schlack had not counted on the time they have to spend teaching their students how to use technology. In this sense, the technology has been a disappointment. In other ways, however, the technology has made important contributions. By making it possible for students to generate more idealized data from simulations, physics software makes it easier for students to see patterns and relationships among variables. Arnashus notes that students tend to "become more experimental" and to ask more "what if" questions when working with technology. Rather than just completing the steps required in an assignment, they start experimenting with the variables in the simulation to explore effects and interactions. Schlack states, "Technology has enabled me to do things I've never been able to do [before] in my teaching." She also appreciates the fact that the technology skills students gain in the process are transferable to other tasks and later life ("it opens up so many opportunities").

Each of the thirteen units Arnashus and Schlack have designed follows a similar structure. The variety of activities within each unit gives students the opportunity to explore, guess, gather data, detect and correct errors, and communicate their findings. Each unit opens with students going to the Internet to search for answers to a set of motivating questions (e.g., "Find an example of damage done by lightning"). Students go to the Media Center for this portion of the unit. Arnashus and Schlack report that they themselves are not proficient with search engines but that with Snow's help they can make sure that their students gain these skills.

Physics labs involve eight to ten activity stations where students explore phenomena and answer questions concerning their observations and the variables underlying the observed phenomena. Typically, one or more of the activity stations is computer based. Students work in groups of three or four to complete the activities. A structured lab report is required for each activity. In the Acceleration and Gravity unit, for example, three of the eight activity stations employ sensors or a photogate. One of the three has a sensor connected to a computer so that the data are graphed immediately; at the other stations, students do the graphing manually. The advantage of the technology is apparent in comparing the computer-based station with manual stations. At one activity station, for example, students use a mechanical launcher to launch a ball at a specified angle. Students observe the ball and use a meter stick on the table to see how far it travels at each of the specified angles. Given the limitation of human ability to judge distance of a moving object with the naked eye, the students' graphed data were full of "noise." Realizing that their resulting data did not form a curve with any definable shape, one group became frustrated and began hypothesizing bogus explanatory variables such as greater air resistance at some angles.

Students' comments to the researchers show that they themselves believe it is easier to discern patterns when working in a computer environment.

> Data's more accurate [when computer-generated]. Well, when we do the labs ourselves, and like write it down with meter sticks and whatever . . . it's a lot less accurate so it's harder to get the point you're trying to get from the data you have. Whereas with the computer, it's all like perfectly exactly what you want to see.

We went on computers and used like programs that would model equations we've done instead of doing them by hand. You could actually see what goes on in there, so it's more interesting.

With only eight computers for the two physics classrooms, the number of activities that can be done on computer is limited by the small amount of classroom technology. The equipment and software in the physics lab were paid for from the school's state Chapter I pool. Arnashus and Schlack wrote a proposal for their principal and local school council describing what they needed and how they would use it. Given their teaching loads of five classes and 140 students a day each, these teachers feel that they have limited time to devote to activities such as exploring new uses of technology or writing proposals to outside funding sources to try to gain resources for additional equipment.

Technology Use in Biology and Physiology Classes

Biology teacher Linda Patton has been teaching at Von Steuben, where she did her student teaching, for four years. Patton has a master's degree in laboratory science and worked in a laboratory for a number of years before going back to school for a master's in education and entering the teaching profession. Patton started using technology while earning her education degree at Northwestern University, where one of her professors was Brian Reiser, a researcher in learning technology. Patton has made her freshman biology classroom available to Reiser as a research site for prototyping a software program on evolution called BGuILE. BGuILE presents students with data and has them generate hypotheses and gather evidence concerning evolutionary patterns. It includes many opportunities for students to analyze data. In addition to the software, Northwestern contributed computer equipment and the assistance of graduate students to support implementation of the program.

Students in Patton's North Park Biology class are taking a course in tandem with students from nearby North Park College. Patton plans the class in collaboration with the North Park faculty member. Because students use a college textbook for this class, they are screened not only on the basis of their freshman biology teacher's recommendation but also on the basis of their reading scores. In practice, the Von Steuben students often outperform their college classmates. Patton describes these students as "the best and the brightest." They come into the lab on their own time and e-mail her with questions at home over the weekend because they do not want to wait until Monday for the answers.

A variety of technology supports this class. Health restrictions, for example, preclude having students work with real blood, so Patton uses prepared slides either on the overhead projector or on a scope cam: "Until they [students] see the slides themselves, it isn't real." Patton uses a laser disk to provide three-dimensional diagrams of organisms and protein structures. Students self-diagnose areas where they need further study and complete tutorials in the corresponding subject areas on a CD-ROM called A.D.A.M. Interactive Physiology (by Benjamin/Cummings). Students frequently use Excel spreadsheets to organize and display their data. Patton can count on their facility with the graphing software derived from their math classes. Patton feels that eliminating the requirement to hand-plot data speeds up the acquisition of concepts.

Diane Gazda (from the Computer Science Department), Randy Snow, and Lucja Kowalski all have provided Patton with assistance at one time or another when she was doing special technology-supported projects with her classes. Patton feels that such special projects take at least two teachers because of the combination of technical and content issues that can arise.

Making a Lab-Based Technology Infrastructure Work

In 1998–99 Von Steuben's three hundred computers gave it a student-to-computer ratio of 5:1, somewhat better than the national average. Most of the equipment, however, was located in one of the school's seven networked laboratories. (In addition to the Writing Center and the Media Center, there were four general computer labs and a CAD lab featuring the latest commercial version of Autocad software.) With just fifty computers distributed among Von Steuben's thirty-five regular classrooms, teachers and students were highly dependent on the labs for technology access.

Several factors helped explain this distribution of the technology. The high cost of wiring in a building as old as Von Steuben's was a major consideration. At one point, the principal had $120,000 he had hoped to spend on wiring the school for technology. The principal then learned that this budget would support only the installation of a backbone, just the start of what would be needed to provide full classroom connectivity. Significant additional costs would be incurred to do the upgrading of electrical systems needed to comply with changed building codes and to replace the lead paint that would be exposed when holes were made for wires.

Uncertainty concerning how much wiring and capital improvement work the district might support led also to caution concerning use of discretionary funds. At the time of our case study, Gazda was aware of the CPS plan to provide support from district-level E-rate funds. The district plan called for connecting ten classrooms and one lab in each high school to the T-1 line and for paying for the needed electrical wiring. Gazda did not want to use precious discretionary funds for things the district would be willing to pay for in the near future.

In addition to cost considerations, there are positive reasons for the laboratory-based strategy. Given the initial lack of familiarity of many teachers with technology, the availability of the human resources of Kowalski and Snow to go along with the technology has been a major advantage. Teachers can begin implementing technology with students at a much earlier stage in their own technology education if they have colleagues to assist them in planning and implementation. Gazda has been prudent in selecting laboratory directors who view themselves as there to work with teachers in improving teaching and learning rather than just to keep the equipment and network running.

Although limited by the constraints of time and scheduling, as are teachers at most schools, Von Steuben teachers appear to have a culture of collaboration. No one at the school credited technology with creating that culture, but certainly the expectation of coordination and cooperation among staff has helped to make the technology work. In addition to the ongoing collaborations supported by the Writing Center and Media Center directors, we saw evidence that teachers in general communicate with each other and pool resources. During the course of one site visit, several teachers mentioned concern about students' acceptance of information they find on the Internet as true and accurate without adequate double-checking or investigation of the information source. During the same visit, Lucja Kowalski shared information she had gathered on this issue with science teacher Carl Shaumberg and explained her intent to disseminate this material to all the teachers. The U.S. history teacher Mary Beth Brandt dropped into the Writing Center that same day bringing some material she had found through U.S. History Day about evaluating Web sites with historical material. Randy Snow later described his preference for increasing use of database subscriptions rather than commercial Web search engines. Clearly Von Steuben teachers worry about the quality of their program, discuss concerns with each other, and share strategies and resources.

The apparent importance of teacher-to-teacher collaboration in making technology work at this urban high school is not an isolated incident. In a 1998 national survey of technology use in education, Becker (1999) found that one of the strongest predictors of amount of Internet technology use is the extent to which teachers collaborate with their peers within their school. By building opportunities and supports for collaboration, the principal is supporting technology implementation as well.

Creating a Supportive Culture for Technology Use

Some of the factors that make Von Steuben a positive environment for students and teachers are central to the school's identity and difficult to reproduce quickly. The school has a tradition of offering a strong program and attracts an above-average student body and faculty. Maintaining its reputation and ability to attract students and staff, however, is an ongoing challenge that is never far from the principal's mind. Next we discuss strategies Gazda has used to encourage the infusion of technology into Von Steuben's program.

Setting an example. Principal Gazda himself has a technology background, which gives him a level of comfort in discussing technology infrastructure with his technology coordinator or arranging for technology training for his staff. Although he does not think a principal needs to have technology skills to promote technology use within the school, he himself sets a good example. Several years ago he learned to use PowerPoint so that he could prepare a multimedia presentation for his teachers on the use of technology. He again used this software in personally developing the Von Steuben presentation for the 1999 Chicago Schools Fair where prospective parents get acquainted with the option schools they might want to choose for their children. In the summer of 1999 Gazda took a two-day Web design class through DeVries to prepare himself to contribute to the school's Web site.

Acquainting teachers with productivity tools. Gazda's first step in stimulating technology use at Von Steuben was undertaken while he was still assistant principal. He trained interested teachers in how to use word processing and spreadsheets to support their own work. Gazda arranged with the district to get "lane placement" (credit toward advancement to a higher pay scale) for this initial course, a move Gazda believes was important in drawing teachers to the course. When teachers found out through the course that word processing could help them save versions of their tests from prior years for easy revision and that spreadsheets could help with grading, they got interested in technology.

Most Von Steuben teachers have chosen to keep their grades on spreadsheets. Teachers like Linda Patton report that this practice significantly enhances their use of time: "Most of us do our grades on a spreadsheet. . . . I put my kids' grades up every week. . . . It's never 'Why'd I get a D? What's this?' . . . I don't have any of that because it's out there every single day. So that's technology that helps me tremendously." Beginning in 1999–2000 Gazda required all teachers to use grading software for posting and reporting grades.

Every Von Steuben teacher we spoke with uses electronic mail for communication. Many participate in listservs for their teaching specialty.

Providing encouragement and support. Gazda has continued the style of his predecessor as principal in encouraging teachers to take risks and providing supports for enhancing their professional skills. This atmosphere is apparent in Lucja Kowalski's description of how she came to take on running the Writing Center. "The administration has got to be there to support you. That was the principal before Rich Gazda, and he was all for it [creating the Writing Center]. He said, 'Go for it, Lucy. Whatever you need, let me know.' So he trusted me." Another teacher commented: "There's been a lot of incentives here to try things, innovations, ideas. Teachers are listened to."

In addition to the hardware, software, and human infrastructure for technology use, to be described further, Gazda gives each department their own technology budget (out of state Chapter I funds). The local school council has approved use of $30,000 of Chapter I funds for technology support costs. Departments write proposals to the school's teacher committee, which then prioritizes requests.

The school council also has approved $10,000 of discretionary funds to support teacher attendance at conferences and in-service trainings. Gazda encourages staff to take advantage of training opportunities involving the use of technology.

Choosing staff. Gazda views the hiring of a few energetic, computer-savvy teachers to act as the catalyst for technology implementation as a key strategy. Having done this at Von Steuben (e.g., in hiring Randy Snow), Gazda takes into account technology facility, and certainly willingness to try using technology, when hiring any new staff. He views the principal's right to select staff on the basis of merit (rather than the calculation of seniority within the district) as the biggest benefit of the Chicago school reform effort.

Although some of the teachers most resistant to trying to use technology are nearing retirement, new, young teachers applying for jobs are not necessarily well prepared to teach with technology, according to Gazda. He notes that the applicants he sees typically are accustomed to using basic productivity tools for their own work but have not been trained to use technologies in supporting teaching and learning within their particular subject area: "Now one of the things I find especially interesting . . . new teachers, they're not really prepared [to use technology in instruction]. They know the word processor somewhat. They're confident with a spreadsheet, but when you ask 'How would you use this with kids?' they never had a class with anyone giving them ideas on how you incorporate that tool into the curriculum area."

Technology support staff. Gazda has taken pains to do what he can to provide the staff needed to support technology use at Von Steuben. In addition to Kowalski and Snow, whose roles were described earlier, Von Steuben is supported by a technology coordinator, Bob Bednar. Bednar, Rich Gazda, and Gazda's wife, Diane, were all involved in Chicago's early computer education efforts during the late 1960s and early 1970s. Bednar left CPS for private industry but was recruited back to take on the Von Steuben position. Although it seems reasonable to expect that a school with seventy-five teachers and fourteen hundred students would have a full-time technology coordinator, most Chicago high schools do not have one. Bednar is responsible for maintenance, technology planning, implementation of the technology plan, and grant proposals. He also handles freshman admissions and the business office. Bednar's position is funded through the regular teacher salary budget but supplemented by state Chapter I funds.

Bednar is supported by two interns who work twenty hours a week each to help maintain the school's LANs. He also has three Von Steuben students who work after school to repair computers, as well as an outside employee who works twenty hours a week. Even so, technology proficient teachers such as Kowalski, Snow, and Diane Gazda do much of their own maintenance and end up helping other teachers with troubleshooting day-to-day problems. "We're really short on technical assistance. We have the tech director, but he seems to be overwhelmed with everything. He has some part-time people working and helping him out. But I still maintain my own equipment. I've gone to troubleshooting classes for both Macintosh and Windows machines so I can understand both."

In part, the heavy local need for maintenance support is the result of decentralization within CPS. Whereas formerly the district had maintenance contracts and equipment could be sent out for repair, now schools must arrange and finance their own maintenance.

Von Steuben also receives considerable support from its TRN consultant (district-level technology coordinator), Dennis Hart. Although Von Steuben shares its TRN with more than twenty other schools, the fact that their TRN is a former Von Steuben employee who helped to install the school's network means that there are strong ties. Bednar and Hart speak on a weekly basis. Hart provides advice on equipment and network configuration and keeps Von Steuben apprised of district policies and opportunities for training and other supports.

Promoting a culture of coordination and mutual support. In summing up Von Steuben's strengths, a teacher commented, "The collaboration is the key factor here."

In contrast to staff at many high schools, those at Von Steuben not only talk to each other but also feel that they can call on each other for assistance, especially in the area of technology use. The cultural norm is to help each other, and to do so rapidly. When

Linda Patton wanted to use the distance learning equipment to connect her anatomy and physiology students with an area physician, for example, "I put that note in Bob's [the technology coordinator] box yesterday, and he's very supportive as I mentioned Randy [the media center director] is. And Lucy Kowalski in the Writing Center. They'll just bend over backwards to support your classes, your projects, and your ideas, and what not. I put a note in Bob's box about the lecture series, you know, 'Can we do that?' and within an hour, next time he came out, he said, 'Great. We're registered.' He'd already taken care of it."

To help ease scheduling problems with the Writing and Media Centers and to encourage research assignments across the curriculum, Gazda brought his department chairs together at the end of the 1998–99 school year to plan for the next year. They decided to collaborate with the Computer Education Department so that time in its courses could be used to support research projects in students' other classes. Instead of learning computer skills using arbitrary exercises, students would be able to gain technology skills as they worked on projects for their other classes.

Barriers to Supporting Instruction with Technology

At each of the urban case study schools, one of the areas we investigated was the obstacles to technology use related to the fact that the school is part of a large urban district. Von Steuben was typical of urban schools with respect to some barriers and atypical with respect to others.

Pressure from an Accountability System

Von Steuben is in a district with one of the strongest accountability systems in the nation. Although the performance bar is set at a low level (at least 15 percent of students performing at or above national standards on basic skills tests), Chicago schools whose students do not meet the standard are subject to reconstitution and staff termination. In addition, the district has imposed not only curriculum standards for each high school core course but also an end-of-course examination aligned with those standards (the CASE exams).

In many schools, such accountability systems are having a chilling effect on innovative uses of technology. Teachers are fearful of devoting too much time to having students explore simulations of science phenomena or performing Internet research, for example, if the content is not tied to the examinations on the basis of which they will be judged.

Von Steuben teachers are sensitive to the district's curriculum requirements. Teacher after teacher talked about covering the required curriculum and using the district standards in their planning. Most seem to feel, however, that the required curriculum leaves adequate room for elaboration and expansion. An English teacher who has participated in a Northwestern University project involving having students design their own culture and develop a Web page describing that culture, for example, explains how he can implement this project while still meeting district requirements.

> I guess for me it's not as difficult because the English curriculum is kind of open when it comes to the Chicago Board of Education and what we're expected to have on these tests. And right now the big thing is the CASE exams. *Romeo and Juliet* is the first semester, along with three shorter nonfiction works. . . . It's not a lot. We can cover that in a quarter. We can get all that stuff done. Second quarter is even easier, *The Pearl*, a short novel we're going to read in about a week, and then just basic terms that we learn all year around. So if you structure the year—this takes a lot of organization and a lot of forethought—but if you structure the year, and you say, "Third quarter we're going to spend a lot of time on Internet stuff," it goes very well.

Von Steuben teachers do not feel pressured to focus on basic reading and mathematics skills in preparation for the state examinations because their students perform well in these areas. (Among Von Steuben eleventh graders, 60 percent score at or above the national norm in reading comprehension and 69 percent at or above the national norm in mathematics.) Most Chicago schools do not have this luxury, however. District TRN consultants note that those schools on "academic watch" have little interest in thinking about the implementation of technology.

Lack of Infrastructure and Funding

In many urban schools, federal Title I compensatory funds are helping to underwrite the costs of technology. Because Von Steuben's students are not high in need relative to its district, the school does not receive federal Title I funds. Most of the discretionary funds available to Von Steuben come from the state Chapter I program, and half of these are consumed by the costs of providing security. Remaining funds support a teacher position, the departmental technology budgets, and teacher professional development costs, among other items. State regulations preclude using Chapter I discretionary funds for capital improvement, however, and Von Steuben's physical facility is in need of expensive renovation if it is to have a modern technology infrastructure.

Although the bulk of Von Steuben's computers are relatively current, the cabling and network components were described by Bednar in 1998 as at the "end of life." Electrical power to the building and floors had been upgraded but most individual classrooms still lacked a power supply adequate to support networked computers. The school's educational technology plan, developed by Bednar with the assistance of local school council members, staff, parents, and other community stakeholders, was described as "conservative" in light of budget constraints. Even so, the plan's executive summary cautioned that the proposed year 1999–2000 infrastructure with Internet connections to ten regular classrooms would not be possible without a significant infusion of external funds.

Another problem is sheer lack of space. The school has plans (outlined later) for several additional computer labs but has no place to put them. (In fact, the school is so crowded that a certain proportion of students must remain in the gymnasium at all times, necessitating spending a good portion of precious discretionary funds on hiring extra physical education teachers.) Space within individual classrooms is an issue also. Today's desktop computers take up significant amounts of room, and when classes are crowded with students, there is simply no place to put more equipment even if it is available. Those teachers most involved in using technology for instruction, such as Linda Patton, feel the pinch the most.

> I need more space for computers right here in the classroom because I really don't like to schlep the kids down to another place if I don't have to. . . . When the kids finish a lab, it's nice if they can turn around . . . and enter their data into a computer. So I had six of them [students] up here, and I sent the rest of them downstairs, which means I had to have an aide to help me because I can't be two places at the same time. So I'd like to have more hardware in the classroom.

It is unclear where the resources for strengthening Von Steuben's technology infrastructure will come from. The school has received only limited support from business in the past. Although they are a desirable site for demonstrating new technologies, such demonstrations have typically provided only limited, very focused resources. Chicago's share of the state's Chapter I funds has been held steady, which has meant declining funds for Von Steuben as the number of low-income students within the school system has risen (forcing a drop in the per-student allocation in order to hold the total constant). Gazda hopes the district will return to an earlier allocation scheme in which the district had schools write proposals for funds, because he believes his staff would fare well in the grants competition. Despite the uncertainty regarding funding sources, Von Steuben is continuing to refine and move forward wherever possible with its technology plan. Principal leadership and creativity clearly will be necessary to identify new funding sources and hold all the pieces together.

Plans

Gazda does not expect to be able to wire all of Von Steuben's classrooms, but he is trying to obtain resources to wire four classrooms per floor. There are forty-two classrooms in the school including the computer labs. Using a combination of district improvement funds, school E-rate funds, and school discretionary funds, Gazda expects to achieve this selective wiring of classrooms. This plan would give each academic department access to a classroom with extensive technology on a scheduled basis.

When the middle school moves out of Von Steuben's building (as expected within the next two years), Gazda hopes to add two new computer laboratories—one for high-end users and one for language instruction. The high-end lab space would take some of the pressure off the Media Center. Gazda hopes the new space will also provide room for departmental offices. He hopes to provide office space with references, inspection textbooks, and other resources relevant to the particular discipline. Each office would have a facsimile machine, an Internet-connected computer, voice mail, and e-mail. He envisions these offices as a place where teachers will do their planning and find many more opportunities to talk to and collaborate with each other. Realizing the importance of such day-to-day informal contact in creating an environment in which teachers continue to learn and grow professionally, Gazda enthuses, "Staff development will go on without my having to pay for it!"

A Final Note

Back when he was assistant principal, Gazda began attending meetings of the North Suburban Shared Technology Consortium (NSSTC), a group of technology coordinators and teachers from districts in the Chicago suburbs. NSSTC membership is composed largely of highly rated schools drawing from economically privileged communities, such as New Trier and the Glenbrook high schools. When asked in what ways implementing technology at Von Steuben was harder than for his fellow NSSTC members at affluent suburban schools, Gazda replies "It's only harder because we don't get the dollars."

Clearly the constant struggle to locate financial resources is a never-ending burden. But Gazda's response is as important for what he did not say as for what he did. Whereas many teachers and administrators in schools serving low-income students have serious doubts about their students' ability to pursue advanced work with technology (Means & Golan, 1998), Gazda sees no such limitations. He views Von Steuben as a school with good students and a committed, talented staff. As principal, he needs to find the resources and create the environment for professional growth that will enable the continuing improvement of the academic program with supports from current technology.

5

Like a Family

TECHNOLOGY'S ROLE IN A PROGRESSIVE HIGH SCHOOL

In the once-infamous Horner Homes area of Chicago's Near West Side, an experiment in public secondary education is unfolding in the shape of Best Practice High School. With fewer than five hundred students, interdisciplinary thematic instruction, and teacher leadership, Best Practice is a radical departure from the typical urban public high school. Richard Riley, former Secretary of Education, could have had Best Practice High School in mind as his model when he called for changing the American high school to fit the needs of today's youth and today's society:

> High school teachers . . . have to be given the opportunity to raise their professional standards. They have to be masters of their field whether it is history, physics, technology or music. . . . I also believe that we need to find ways to create small, supportive learning environments that give students a sense of connection. That's hard to do when we are building high schools the size of shopping malls. . . . We can create schools-within-schools . . . and make sure that every high school student has an adviser for all four years that the student can count on all the time.

> (U.S. Department of Education, September 15, 1999)

Because Best Practice possesses many of the features education reformers advocate as strategies for improving student adjustment and achievement (Lee, Smith, & Croninger, 1995), studying this high school allows us to examine the role of technology in the context of a restructured school.

School Origins

Urban redevelopment and education reform forces came together to spawn Best Practice, which opened in the fall of 1996. The school's Near West Side neighborhood is one formerly best known for the dangerous, decaying Horner Homes federal housing project. Community leader Alex Polikoff, director of Business and Professional People for the Public Interest (BPI), argued that the area was too unsafe for human habitation and was instrumental in getting a U.S. district court decision requiring the Chicago Housing Authority to replace high-rise public housing with dispersed, subsidized town homes. A concentrated effort to redevelop Chicago's Near West Side area, including building the United Center sports arena (where the Bulls play) and putting in new streets and parks, went hand in hand with building low-rise housing attractive to multiple income groups. Leaders behind the neighborhood redevelopment realized the need to improve the educational resources in the area and turned to groups such as Chicago's Leadership for Quality Education (LQE), led by John Ayers, for assistance.

The scheduling of the 1996 Democratic National Convention for the United Center sports arena gave a sense of urgency to the community's call for school renovation. The closest high school, Cregier Vocational, had closed in June 1995 after earning notoriety as "one of the abysmal schools that helped give Chicago its national reputation as an educational disaster zone" (Poe, 1996). In addition to problems with violence, the school suffered from neglect of its physical infrastructure. The building had gone for nearly thirty years without being painted and lacked enough power to start the boilers. The Chicago Public Schools (CPS) decided to thoroughly renovate the Cregier building to make it a showpiece for the Chicago educational reform. A deal was made to rent out the school building as the site for the convention press center. Major renovation of the interior and exterior gave the old building a new, cared-for look.

At the time this renovation effort was getting under way, the CPS was interested in education reform research showing the effectiveness of small schools. A district task force solicited proposals for small schools with distinctive characters or themes.

John Ayers made the connection between the Near West Side neighborhood's goals and those of education reformers at National Louis University (located in nearby Evanston). National Louis was seeking a test bed where it could implement the school reform ideas of its Center for City Schools faculty. National Louis faculty members Steve Zemelman, Harvey ("Smokey") Daniels, and Marilyn Bizar were promoting a "best practice" model with thirteen interlocking characteristics: student-centered, experiential, holistic, authentic, expressive, reflective, social, collaborative, democratic, cognitive, developmental, constructivist, and challenging. Zemelman and Daniels reasoned in *Best Practice: New Standards for Teaching and Learning in America's Schools*, their 1993 book written with Arthur Hyde, that these characteristics run throughout the standards for teaching and learning promoted by the major national professional organizations such as the National Council of Teachers of Mathematics, the National Council of Teachers of English, the American Association for the Advancement of Science, and the National Council for the Social Studies.

Use of modern technology was not one of the characteristics included in the model promoted by National Louis, but many theorists have argued that the kind of student-centered approach these university researchers promote is highly compatible with students' active use of technology tools (Means & Olson, 1995). Central Park East High School, a school considered as a model by the founders of Best Practice, makes extensive use of technology (Rosenfeld, 1991).

Through his work with the Illinois Writing Project, Harvey Daniels had become acquainted with Tom and Kathy Daniels, two Chicago English teachers who shared with Daniels not only a last name but also a belief in the student-centered best-practice approach to education. This husband and wife team (no relation to Harvey Daniels) had been teaching in the Chicago school system for more than thirty years and had grown increasingly frustrated with what they viewed as the dehumanizing environment schools had become for teachers and students alike. The Daniels were recruited as teacher leaders for the new effort. They worked with the National Louis faculty to write a proposal for a new school and to seek both foundation funding and approval and a school site from the Chicago School Board. The Best Practice proposal was eventually chosen by the Board as one of three small, innovative schools to share the Cregier building.

School Character

Best Practice opened in the fall of 1996 with 140 ninth graders, a principal, six teachers (math, science, English, history, art, physical education), one librarian, one special education teacher but—as an unfortunate by-product of the rushed preparations—no books, desks, or computers. According to principal Sylvia Gibson, Ameritech moved out on a Sunday, school staff moved in that Monday, and they had students on Tuesday. Best Practice became the first new public high school to open in Chicago in over twenty years.

As the original class of students has advanced in grade, a new class of students has been added during each year of Best Practice's operation. During the first year of our case study the school had 374 students in grades 9 through 11. The school's plan is to remain small, with a targeted size of five hundred once all four grades are in operation (school year 1999–2000).

Best Practice is heterogeneous and untracked by design. A majority (75 percent) of the school's students come from a network of fourteen "feeder" K–8 schools around the city that have been working with National Louis University. These students thus come from programs with a similar philosophy and instructional approach. The other 25 percent of students come from the surrounding neighborhood and from other parts of the city. Students from all sources are picked through a lottery.

Best Practice does not select students on the basis of grades or test scores per se, but several features of the application and review procedure tend to produce a student body with a higher-than-average level of motivation. Students and their parents must complete five-page application forms explaining why the students would like to attend Best Practice and why their parents would like for them to attend. A teacher or counselor reference and attendance and test score information are required. Students who are chronic truants are eliminated from the applicant pool. Special education students with learning disabilities are accepted in the lottery pool and make up 10 percent of the student body; these students are fully mainstreamed into classes with other students. The school strives for a 50:50 gender balance and for equal proportions of African American and Latino students (just 4 percent of the student body are white non-Hispanic or Asian). More than 80 percent of Best Practice's students come from homes with incomes low enough to qualify them for free or reduced-price lunch.

Tom Daniels says that Best Practice appeals to parents because it is small and safe. "We don't tolerate gang activity or violence." Tom draws an analogy between the urban redevelopment movement from large housing projects to low-rise scattered housing and the educational movement from large, impersonal "shopping mall" high schools to small, distinctive schools like Best Practice.

Sylvia Gibson serves as principal for all three of the schools in the Cregier multiplex. She handles administrative, physical plant, lunch room, and custodial staff issues. Tom and Kathy Daniels, as Best Practice's "lead teachers," orchestrate the activities of their fellow teachers with respect to teaching and learning issues.

All of Best Practice's teachers applied to work at this school and were screened for their commitment to the Best Practice philosophy. Best Practice staff interview prospective new teachers and make hiring recommendations to the principal. Through this process, they are able to maintain a close-knit professional and social community. "It's like a family," comments Tom Daniels.

Traditional education quality indicators suggest that something about the Best Practice approach is having positive effects. Despite the fact that students commute from all over the city, Best Practice enjoys an attendance rate of 93 percent compared with the city average of 91.5 percent. The mobility rate at Best Practice (number of students who enroll or leave the school during the year) is 14.7 percent compared with 28.5 percent for CPS as a whole. Less than 1 percent of Best Practice students are classified as chronic truants compared with 4.4 percent in the district as a whole. At 10 percent, the school's dropout rate is well below the city average of 16 percent.

Although Best Practice had not yet had a graduating class at the time of our case study, its test scores for ninth and tenth graders were considerably above city averages. On the 1997–98 Illinois Goal Assessment Program, 53 percent of Best Practice tenth graders met or exceeded state standards in reading (compared to 48 percent districtwide) and 62 percent met or exceeded standards in math (cf. 56 percent across the district). Among Chicago's seventy-four high schools, Best Practice ninth and tenth graders ranked fourteenth in mathematics and twenty-second in reading on the Test of Academic Proficiency (TAP). Since many of the top-ranking Chicago high schools use selective admissions, National Louis University faculty argue that these scores put Best Practice fifth or sixth among Chicago high schools that do not admit students on the basis of test scores (National Louis University, 1997, p. 1).

One of the more unusual features of Best Practice is its concept of a "negotiated curriculum." The teaching staff is very committed to providing a rigorous program that prepares all students for college. At the same time, the Best Practice philosophy includes relating to student interests. Teachers run focus groups composed of sixteen or seventeen students at the end of each academic year to try to gain an appreciation of the issues about which students care the most. Students discuss the questions they have about themselves and their world. Best Practice faculty consider these student concerns and interests when doing their curriculum planning for the next year.

Best Practice staff are sensitive also to other feedback from their students. Students applaud the school's diversity and social community as well as its academics, but some express concern that because of the school's small size and unique nature they miss out on many of the extracurricular activities that larger schools offer. One student even wrote a note suggesting that Best Practice set aside a day a week to function "like a normal high school." On our first visit to the school we observed one faculty response to this concern as a teacher bustled from class to class posting pink notices for cheerleader tryouts.

Features of the Best Practice Experience

Best Practice uses a complicated schedule to accommodate traditional, academically rigorous classes, extended interdisciplinary units, and external internships. All students have six classes. On Mondays and Fridays, students have a fifty-minute period for each class. Tuesdays and Thursdays feature three one-hundred-minute blocks, with each class getting one of these extended periods on one of the two days. These extended blocks are used also for the integrated thematic units. On Wednesdays, freshmen and sophomores have internships from 8:30 to 11:55 A.M. and "Choice" from 1:40 to 2:50 P.M. Best Practice teachers provide a wide range of Choice options, ranging from extra help on homework to clubs, holiday arts and crafts activities, board games, and invited speakers. Each day also includes a thirty-minute "advisory" between students and their assigned teacher advisers. In most cases, students stay with the same adviser throughout their careers at Best Practice. During the advisories, students discuss problems and teachers keep track of their progress. Advisories have the explicit goal of building close relationships between students and teachers as a way of both minimizing disorderly behavior and catching potential personal and academic problems before they become intractable. Kathy Daniels calls the advisories "our first line of defense," and Tom adds, "We work as hard as we can to make sure no one falls through the cracks."

The student internships at Best Practice are designed to be part of a four-year sequence that will help students explore personal talents and goals, find direction for further education and work, acquire job and social skills, and find satisfaction in helping others. All students attend a September Job Fair where they select five internship sites of interest and write an essay about what they like about each. Many of the freshman students get internships in elementary schools where they serve as teachers' aides. A program with Loyola University Child Law Center has Best Practice students playing the role of witnesses in practice sessions with law students. Other examples of internships include entering data for a community organization, working at a Web site development company, and producing large photo murals for a photo lab. Some students attend classes at nearby Malcolm X College in lieu of the internship. Classes students have taken include PowerPoint and Allied Health. Students are required to keep a weekly journal of their internship experiences and are evaluated by their job supervisors three times a year.

Each year, Best Practice teachers for each grade level work as a group to plan four to five integrated curriculum units around themes representing student and teacher interests. One of the first multidisciplinary units was "Here We Are," an extended exploration of their 1902 school building's history and architecture as well as a study of the history and community of the Near West Side. Another unit on "isms" (e.g., racism, sexism, ageism) had each student spending two weeks studying one of these forms of prejudice, searching for patterns of causation, and looking for ways to solve conflicts. At the end of each extended unit, students make public presentations of their work. One girl commented on the value of such long-term projects:

> I think that the only hard thing was the amount of time you had to put into it. . . . It's school work, you have to do it, even if you don't want to. I think it's, like, an opportunity. Because like when you get out in the real world, you're going to have to start stuff that's like even harder than this. You can use it as an opportunity to learn how to work out stuff and manage your time. You have to figure out how to manage your time and get it done. So I think it's worth it.

The close relationship between Best Practice students and their teachers is apparent in the classrooms. Douglas Spalding's chemistry class, for example, is a far cry from the typical high school science class where the teacher lectures and students listen with varying degrees of attention, taking notes verbatim without necessarily understanding what the terms or concepts mean. Spalding runs a much more interactive small class. He continually elicits student input and does not move off a topic until the students exhibit understanding. He makes sure that students are seated in chairs where he can see their faces; sometimes he will touch a shoulder to capture attention; he himself speaks with energy and expressive body language.

As we watched, Spalding posted a realistic problem for the consideration of his sophomore students. "50 L of heating oil spills on a lake creating an oil slick 500,000 cm^2 in area. Estimate the thickness of the oil." Several students expressed uncertainty about the unit of measurement to use for the answer. Spalding asked, "How do we get from L/cm^2 to something like cm?" A student suggested doing some cancellations and conversions, and Spalding assented but pushed for more. "Sounds like a good idea. Help me out. How do we measure volume in something like cm?" A student interjected, "I've got a question," and Spalding attended to her confusion before pressing on. "Joy, are you ready?" Joy responded, "I'm ready." Spalding pushed her for a suggestion, "What goes on top (of the equation)? What goes on the bottom?" Joy responded eagerly and confidently. Spalding complimented her: "You guys are too smart today." Spalding could tell from some students' faces that they did not follow Joy's line of reasoning, however. "Hold on. Don't let this slide by." He passed out sugar cubes to the students. "How big is that?" (A sugar cube is about one centimeter on each side, thus a cubic centimeter.) As the students worked through the measurement units and conversions, Spalding provided encouragement, "This example is a lot like one you have to do on your homework," and "The first rule of solving problems is common sense." Spalding spent much more time on the problem than the typical chemistry teacher would. When he finished, the observers felt confident that most if not all of the students understood the problem and could solve something comparable on their homework or a test.

The Technology Infrastructure at Best Practice

In preparation for the 1996 Democratic National Convention, Ameritech put in wiring, cabling, and a T-1 Internet connection to serve the press center housed in the school building. CPS and staff involved in preparing for Best Practice's fall opening contacted Ameritech and convinced them to put in additional wiring for computers and telephones for rooms that would become Best Practice classrooms. Through CPS efforts and Ameritech's donation, Best Practice had 65 percent of its instructional rooms wired for the Internet at a time when relatively few Chicago schools had Internet connections for rooms other than computer labs.

Tom Daniels acted as de facto technology coordinator for his school. Tom saw technology as fitting in with the Best Practice emphasis on "active learning." Daniels did the planning to obtain network and computer equipment and ran Best Practice's laboratory of twenty-one computers. Roughly half of the computers in the laboratory are Macintoshes and half PCs because the teachers were divided in terms of their preferred computing platform. Keeping the lab open from 7:30 A.M. until 4:30 P.M. each school day, Daniels supported teachers when they signed up to use the lab for class activities. He also takes responsibility for trying to keep the network and computers running. Gene Servillo, an external consultant, provides technical support approximately one day a week.

Daniels himself became familiar with computers in the course of process writing staff development. In terms of his technology support role, Daniels confessed, "There's a lot of stuff I didn't know. I'm an English teacher."

By fall of 1998 Best Practice had forty-five computers to serve its 340 students and nineteen teachers. In addition to the twenty-one computers in the laboratory and twenty-four distributed among regular classrooms, there were five laptop computers for teacher use. Tom Daniels estimated that all but four or five Best Practice teachers were comfortable using technology in their teaching.

Best Practice's computer lab computers are on a local area network (LAN) connected to the Internet. The school has a Novell server, capable of supporting diverse platforms (Mac and PC) and providing nine megabytes set aside for each student's work. Rather than using the intranet to its full extent, most computers are connected directly to the Internet via the router because it was easier to set up.

At the beginning of the 1998–99 school year, the T-1 line installed by Ameritech was connected via a router to Whitney Young High School (a much larger, academically selective high school) to provide Best Practice with access to the district and state wide area network (WAN). When there was a problem with the connection, Best Practice had to rely on Whitney Young to fix it. During that year Best Practice received a second T-1 line from CPS as part of the district's commitment to provide every school with Internet access. Unfortunately, no one knew the routing from the router back into the school, and it was nearly the end of the school year before the new T-1 line, which could provide direct access without having to go through Whitney Young, became operational.

The Role of External Partners

Our earlier case studies of schools that pioneered the use of tech-nology as an element of school reform found that most such schools received significant intellectual and financial resources from exter-nal partners (Means & Olson, 1995). Best Practice is a prime exam-ple of how important such external relationships are in helping a school set its vision and support the use of technology related to that vision. National Louis University faculty not only played a piv-otal role in Best Practice's original design and establishment, they have continued to support the school through guest teaching, design of a student peer mediation program, grant writing, help with curriculum planning, recruiting students from the network of feeder schools, staff development offerings, school tour leading, and serving on the local school council. In turn, Best Practice serves as the primary clinical site for National Louis's new secondary Master of Arts in Teaching (M.A.T.) program. Preservice M.A.T. students are able to work in an innovative urban high school.

Although the National Louis University partnership is the most pervasive, Best Practice staff also work with a number of other external organizations that have influenced its program. Best Prac-tice is one of six Chicago area high schools participating in Fermi Lab's Project ARISE (American Renaissance in Science Educa-tion). Leon Lederman, the Nobel laureate physicist who directs Fermi Lab, received a National Science Foundation grant to rework the high school science curriculum. Lederman argues that the tra-ditional sequence of biology, chemistry, and then physics no longer makes sense in an era when biology is more dependent on bio-chemistry and less a matter of classifying organisms. In this "Physics First" curriculum, high school freshmen take physics, followed by chemistry in the sophomore year and biology in the junior year. Lederman explains: "We're proposing a kind of conceptual physics that is not so mathematical, using just the algebra ninth graders know. You can teach Newtonian motion, the conservation of energy, and give a feeling of what an atom is, so they can walk into chemistry the next year with grace and confidence. Having those concepts first seems to be especially helpful for girls and minorities."

In addition to reversing the usual course order, the ARISE curriculum stresses the integration of mathematics and science and an inquiry-based approach to instruction. The only Chicago public school in the project besides Best Practice is the academically selective Whitney Young.

Best Practice has been quite successful in attracting private foundation support for its distinctive programs. Best Practice and its network of feeder schools work with National Louis on teacher development and parent involvement activities funded by the Joyce Foundation and the Chicago Annenberg Challenge grants. The Joyce Foundation and the McDougal Family Foundation have supported summer participation of Best Practice faculty at the Walloon Institute held each summer in Petosky, Michigan. This annual retreat exposes Best Practice staff to ideas from other participating schools and allows them time together to refine their vision for their school, discuss best-practice principles, and plan curriculum.

Technology activities have been supported by two $50,000 grants from the Prince Charitable Trust. The first grant was used to support staff development on technology; the second financed science lab equipment.

Other private foundations that have contributed funding for planning and programming at Best Practice include Polk Brothers Foundation, the Fry Foundation, the Quest Center of the Chicago Teachers Union, the J.C. Penney Foundation, and the DeWitt Wallace Readers Digest Fund.

Best Practice has also received corporate donations. In addition to the network infrastructure provided by Ameritech, Best Practice negotiated a deal to receive software and teacher training from Open Text Corporation. The company pledged to help Best Practice teachers use Open Text software to develop digital portfolios of student work. Best Practice staff have been talking about implementing digital portfolios for several years, but the effort has never really gained momentum. Tom Daniels expressed hope that the provision of this structured software and the associated training in fall of 1999 would provide the necessary impetus. As often happens with school-business partnerships, events transpired to delay the planned activities. The school's contact at Open Text sold the company so only preliminary meetings were held in 1999–2000. Kathy Daniels reported in May 2000 that they still plan to do the project, and Open Text has agreed to train teachers over the summer. The teachers' time would be paid by an Annenberg Challenge grant.

Relations with the Chicago Public Schools

Best Practice has a kind of love-hate relationship with the Chicago district office (Board of Education). Clearly the school does not fit the urban public school mold. The district's interest in promoting small schools, which was high at the time Best Practice was established, is perceived to have waned. Moreover, Best Practice's structure and philosophy run counter to much of what the CPS is promoting as school improvement steps. Where Best Practice believes in inclusion, including its special education students in "trigonometry, physics, everything," CPS actions have resulted in "tracking at the school level" according to Tom Daniels. Daniels decried the district's establishing academically selective magnet schools around the district and to its practice of holding students who score below the eighth-grade level in Bridge programs until a regular high school is willing to accept them.

Although Best Practice staff may not agree with many of the practices promoted by the CPS, the school's teachers draw on their years of experience in the district to find ways of living within the system. Best Practice staff do not ignore the content on the statewide tests Chicago uses for accountability purposes. For several weeks prior to testing each spring, teachers review the content and item formats that will be on the standardized tests. Unlike many of the other small and charter schools started in Chicago in recent years, Best Practice has posted strong test performance for its students and as a consequence has enjoyed considerable freedom in setting its curriculum and instructional approach.

The major area of contention between Best Practice and the district appears to be over resources. Although CPS provided Best Practice with $200,000 for start-up costs, some staff feel the district has not come forward with all the resources it promised. At the time of our case study, Tom Daniels was still smarting from the indignity of having to open the school without desks or textbooks. Often problems arise because the Best Practice model is incompatible with district formulae for funding, time distribution, and so on. For example, district allocation of teaching positions is based on size of enrollment, and with the school's small size, they do not have the numbers to support the three science teachers needed for their program. They have had to scramble to find discretionary and grant funds to support their biology teacher and also lead teachers, who provide instructional vision and leadership for the school. Tom Daniels's position is funded through the state Chapter I funds that Best Practice receives by virtue of the number of low-income students it serves. Kathy Daniels's position was funded because the district was experimenting with small junior and senior academies. Both funding sources are susceptible to fluctuation or even termination.

Sporadic points of friction aside, Best Practice has received some important supports from the CPS. When Tom Daniels was trying to figure out how to equip a modern chemistry lab for Best Practice, he approached the district and learned that as part of the Chicago Systemic Initiative to improve science education, funded by the National Science Foundation, seven Chicago schools would get state-of-the art $500,000 labs. Daniels succeeded in getting Best Practice included as one of the seven schools.

The district has supported technology use at Best Practice not only through provision of a second T-1 line but also through the services of its TRN consultant. Although the district describes the TRN's role as primarily one of training teachers, Best Practice views the TRN's responsibility as providing advice for technology planning. Daniels does not expect the TRN to provide staff development for Best Practice teachers or to provide on-site technical support. Daniels finds the TRN's contribution to technology planning and keeping the school abreast of district developments that could support their technology infrastructure "incredibly helpful." In this case, there is a good match between the school's expectations and what the TRN can provide to any one of the more than twenty schools to which the TRN is assigned.

On the whole, the CPS tolerates Best Practice's unconventionality and provides what it views as appropriate resources. The district does not usually go so far as to provide above-average support, however, and has not tried to leverage the Best Practice approach as an alternative model for urban education. In contrast, BPI leader Alex Polikoff perceives that all of the community schools in the Near West Side are in serious trouble and wants to get Best Practice involved in helping them to change and improve. National Louis University funded visits to Best Practice by network neighborhood schools with the hope that the teachers from the other schools would adopt best practices. Visiting teachers spent time at Best Practice planning how to implement what they had seen there in their own classrooms. Thus, the primary interest in and support for the Best Practice model continue to come from partners outside the public school system, such as National Louis University, Fermi Labs, community groups, and private foundations.

Use of Technology at Best Practice High School

The Best Practice stance toward technology is to have it available as a tool that can support learning in the curriculum areas. Technology skills are not ends in themselves, but technology is one of the media through which students can master the academic content that is the school's mission. Tom Daniels explained, "Be careful to see it [technology] as a tool to get information—to help kids learn—rather than the end itself. We think technology is a part of what we call our multiple intelligence approach. Some kids can't learn through a book, but they like learning through a computer, or might learn through a camera or might learn through art work or something like that."

Most of the use of technology at Best Practice High School exemplifies what has been called the "tool" approach (Means et al., 1993). Relatively little instructional software is used. More common is the incorporation of general-purpose productivity tools, originally developed for use in business and research communities, into classroom assignments. Physics teacher Art Griffin described this view:

> Word processing, the use of word processing, and the power of being able to use a computer to even put together a paper, that is something that our kids need to have, and basically, what is happening, is that . . . all of the teachers—at least here at this school—are taking the kids down [to the computer lab] periodically showing them how to use a word processing program, that is, Claris Works, Microsoft, Word Perfect, and in fact, it is a wonderful thing. Tom Daniels has made sure that we have almost all of the latest word processing programs along with spreadsheets, and they [the students] are learning how to do that. We use spreadsheets in physics. They do graphing on computers too, so, I mean, these are all forms of technology that I think our kids need to be exposed to.

As Tom Daniels became more familiar with the concepts of LANs, he was an early convert, seeing the need for students to be able to access technology and their electronically stored work from any location within the school. Although the school has not yet been able to get the amount of technology it would like to have into instructional classrooms, it does have a network and server with space set aside for students to store their work. This allows students to access their work from any computer on the network and to submit assignments electronically. Students typically use the computer laboratory to complete assignments after regular school hours. They can then leave the finished product in their personal file and send an e-mail message to their teacher with instructions on where to find it. Tom Daniels commented: "Every subject uses computers now. Physics uses Hands-On Universe, the math department uses graphic analysis and spreadsheets, the English department uses word processing, the art department uses it [technology] in a variety of different ways, and there are four integrated curriculum projects per year for each of the grade levels."

Although many Best Practice teachers are incorporating technology into at least some of their assignments, they are generally uncomfortable with the practice of teaching skills outside the context of their use. Hence, no computer literacy, keyboarding, or software classes are taught at Best Practice. Students acquire technology skills in the course of completing assignments that require them. Some teachers believe Best Practice students would benefit from explicit instruction on technology skills, but the state and district requirements that all "vocationally" oriented courses be part of a three-course sequence limits options for an academically oriented school like Best Practice. Tom Daniels interpreted this requirement as a prohibition from offering a single course in technology.

> When the Board separated all of the schools up into college prep and career academy, the tech stuff they automatically stuck into the career academy. So it would be very difficult for me to offer, even if I had the space, remember I only have one room in here. . . . But if I wanted to teach keyboarding, I couldn't teach it. . . . If I wanted to teach PowerPoint I couldn't teach it. Or anything else related to computers. So if they [CPS] are going to have anything as far as proficiency in technology, they wouldn't be asking it of us.

Some Best Practice students enter ninth grade with strong technology skills developed at their elementary schools. Others have virtually no experience in this area. Given the low-income backgrounds of most Best Practice students, they have fewer opportunities than middle-class students do to pick up computer skills at home. The uneven level of technology preparation among Best Practice students means that when a teacher decides to incorporate technology into an assignment, some students will require a significant amount of time to master the technology. Given the limited availability of the computer lab, however, there has been reluctance to provide time there for keyboarding training and little enthusiasm for incorporating keyboarding and word processing training more explicitly into English classes. One of the teachers mentioned the possibility of offering keyboarding practice as a Choice activity.

Although uneven student preparation and limited access to computers have been barriers to technology use among some Best Practice teachers, others have persevered. Two examples illustrate the nature of computer use at the school.

Teaching Perspective Drawing

Veteran art teacher Aiko Boyce has been teaching in and around Chicago for thirty years. She became interested in the use of technology in art in 1983 when she first began exploring graphics programs. At one point she worked at the Communication Art Center sponsored by Disney. While there Aiko not only strengthened her own technology skills but also learned how to plan technology activities that could be completed within the short amount of time students' regular classroom teachers brought them to her center. Aiko was one of the first teachers hired at Best Practice when it opened in 1996. She was attracted to the school because it wanted to do the same kinds of things she had always wanted to do. "It's heaven here."

Aiko teaches five classes of freshman art and is included on the freshman planning team. She often teams up with physics teacher Art Griffin to do units integrating physics concepts and art.

In December 1998, after a monthlong unit on perspective drawing, Aiko brought her freshman art students to the computer laboratory to do two-point perspective drawing using Claris Works

Paint. Aiko wanted her students to transfer the ideas they had discussed in class and practiced with paper and pencil to their work with the Paint program. She believes it is an opportunity for students who do not draw well with paper and pencil to demonstrate their understanding of the concepts in a different medium.

The assignment required students to familiarize themselves with the basic tools in Claris Works Paint (i.e., Line, Rectangle, Oval, Fill, Pencil, and Erase). They then needed to figure out how to use these tools to draw a horizon line and two vanishing points at the beginning and end of the horizon. Finally, students were to use this structure to create four simple objects (e.g., a domino or box of gum) in two-point perspective. The class would have two of the hundred-minute block periods to complete this assignment.

Aiko opened the unit by using the computer connected to a projector on a demonstration equipment cart to review use of Claris Works and the techniques of perspective drawing. Students sat at the center table in the lab with handout sheets explaining the assignments as Aiko went through the demonstration and explanation. She showed students how to open the application, which settings to change (e.g., page orientation, pixel size), and how to save and label their work. She demonstrated use of the Line tool and the Fill tool within Claris Works Paint and encouraged students to experiment.

Students then dispersed to the twenty-one working computers within the computer lab. Several students had to double up because of the limited number of computers. Tom Daniels made himself available during the first part of the class for backup technical support. On the first day, many students had basic technical problems; for example, many did not remember their passwords and needed Tom's help to log on. In contrast, other students appeared comfortable with the Claris Works tools and began making progress on the assignment. One girl, for example, completed an object and tried to color it with the Fill tool. The background filled in also, but the student had enough understanding of the software to diagnose her problem, "A line must be open somewhere."

She zoomed in to find the open spot and used the Pencil tool to fill the gap in the line. She zoomed out and refilled the object correctly. Other students were still hung up on the basic operation of the software.

During the second block period, many fewer students needed technical assistance from Tom Daniels. Only a few had forgotten their passwords or how to log on. All the students created a file without assistance. A half dozen students started experimenting with shapes before creating the required horizon line. A few students responded to a mistake by erasing all of their work rather than just the last function. Some spent time on extraneous features, such as the fill colors or font.

In addition to seeking help from Daniels or Aiko, students got help from their peers on the mechanics of using the software. One group of students conversed quietly in Spanish about the different tools. A student who was having trouble with the Line tool got reminded by his neighbor to hold down the shift key. Another student showed a peer how to draw guidelines for an object to the vanishing points on the horizon line.

Questions addressed to Aiko during the unit were equally divided between those concerning use of the software tools and those concerning two-point perspective drawing. One student needed help drawing perspective guidelines (which are supposed to start from a point on the object and connect to vanishing points on the horizon line). Aiko reminded students of the work they did on this skill in the classroom when they drew windows in two-point perspective. Several times, as Aiko was responding to student requests for assistance, she made sketches on a piece of paper to remind them of earlier in-class activities.

Aiko herself is very comfortable with computer tools and enjoys incorporating technology-based art activities into her class. When she does so, however, she needs to spend significant amounts of time teaching the application as well as the content of her assignment. The amount of time these projects require causes concern also in terms of equitable use of the computer lab. Both Aiko and

Daniels mentioned the need to make sure the art classes do not monopolize the computer lab.

Hands-On Universe

Art Griffin, Best Practice's physics teacher, came to the school from Whitney Young where he taught for ten years. Griffin is active in science education reform efforts in the Chicago area and is committed to finding ways to involve students in real science. He is an active member of the science education community, having participated in training not only for Fermi Lab's Project ARISE but also for Modeling Physics at Arizona State University, the "Hands-on Feet-on Science" program offered by Columbia College for CPS, and the Hands-On Universe Project of University of California, Berkeley's Lawrence Berkeley Lab. Griffin himself has trained teachers through the Adler Planetarium, both in the Chicago area and in Baton Rouge.

The physics lab at Best Practice was remodeled by CPS for the high school's opening. The spacious room, which contains lab tables and work areas, has two computers that Griffin can use for classroom management purposes or for student workstations involving developing graphs or using word processing. Griffin would like to have more technology in his classroom but is limited by a lack of equipment and software he judges to be suitable ("I would say you're probably looking at 75 or 80 percent that is just worthless stuff that they have got out there, and only a small fraction of it that is really good").

Griffin's teaching makes extensive use of sensors and probes, using them for almost every unit, but Griffin has limited capability to give students experiences using probes connected to computers that can display, graph, and store data, given the fact that there are only two computers in his classroom.

One of the major uses of technology in Griffin's class is in support of the Hands-On Universe Project. This project gives students the opportunity to use image processing software to explore and investigate images from a network of automated telescopes. Automated telescopes now capture many more images from outer space than professional astronomers have time to analyze. Hands-On Universe enlists students to review images from space to acquire concepts and skills of research astronomy and help search for supernovas and asteroids. (A Hands-On Universe student group has in fact discovered a previously unknown supernova and had their work published in a scientific journal.) Hands-On Universe enables students to use the same kinds of software tools that scientists use (albeit with more user-friendly interfaces) to examine and classify downloaded images. TERC, a science education curriculum developer, has created instructional materials to accompany the Hands-On Universe software and images.

Griffin uses the Hands-On Universe activities with his class for roughly four weeks, starting around mid-February. Griffin justifies the inclusion of astronomy in his physics course on the grounds that the Illinois State Board of Education says that students should cover seven areas of science, including space science, during high school. The integration of mathematics, chemistry, and physics in the Hands-On Universe activities fits well with Best Practice's interdisciplinary approach. Students get additional practice in algebra, measurement, and the scientific method through this project. Concepts such as light and the color spectrum introduced in the course of analyzing the chemical makeup of stars will be further reinforced in Best Practice students' chemistry course the next year.

In the phase of this project observed by the research team, students were practicing application of a galaxy categorization scheme. They were learning to distinguish stars from galaxies, and new galaxies (likely homes to supernovas) from old galaxies, and to locate "H2" regions associated with nebulae (dust cloud remnants of old supernovas).

We observed a class of twenty-three freshman physics students as they worked on a TERC activity involving detecting features of and classifying galaxies. Working with a handout on galaxy features, students examined a set of galaxies on their computer screens and used software tools to enhance various features in the computer images so that patterns were easier to detect. Students were working in pairs within the computer lab during one of the hundred-minute blocks devoted to physics. Griffin's use of student pairs was motivated both by equipment limitations and by a belief in the virtue of peer collaboration: "A group of two works out pretty well where you may not have enough computers for one per person. And, often times, you know, when you work in a group, one person catches something that the other one doesn't catch, so that they aid each other in a sense of being able to help each other out."

Griffin started the lesson by reviewing critical features of galaxies and projecting some of the computer images provided by Hands-On Universe. As the students examined and classified the eight galaxies in this assignment, they were to check off the features they detected in each and make a sketch of the galaxy as well as making a decision as to galaxy type (e.g., spiral, elliptical, or peculiar).

Students within each pair talked to each other about what manipulations of the computer images to try and what the enhanced images showed. Griffin walked around the room, stopping to talk to various pairs about what they were seeing and what additional tools might be helpful.

Having had about two weeks' experience with the software, students appeared adept at using the Hands-On Universe tools. They changed the colors and brightness of the images, zoomed in to look at specific features, and zoomed out to get an impression of overall shape; they rotated the image to see it from multiple perspectives. However, we saw little use of some of the more-sophisticated features of the software, such as the graphing tool.

As we watched, a pair of girls concentrated on trying to classify Galaxy #6. After manipulating the color of the computer image, they saw a ring that led them to conclude it was a spiral galaxy. Some of the image's other features were inconsistent with this classification, however, and they called Griffin over to discuss their uncertainty and the tools they had tried (brightness levels, shapes, galaxy vs. star diagnosis). Griffin commented, "You can't see the forest for the trees," and urged them to review their data. Griffin pointed to several dark spots on the image and challenged the girls to explain why they were there. Spurred on by Griffin's remarks, the girls conferred further and concluded (correctly) that the galaxy is in fact a spiral galaxy but one with dust lanes (that block light from the galaxy). The bright spots surrounding the galaxy image are stars from our own galaxy and not part of the galaxy being classified.

After seventy minutes, Griffin noted that several of the student groups were only about halfway through the assignment, and he urged them to either write shorter descriptions or make plans to come in after school. Students handed in their papers, which Griffin reviewed quickly before doing a wrap-up summary of galaxy characteristics using a galaxy poster. He concluded with a discussion of the concept of "dark holes." Although the class had extended into eight minutes of the students' lunch period, most of them were still engaged.

Other Teachers' Technology Use

In interviews with SRI researchers, Daniels reported that all but four or five Best Practice teachers were comfortable using technology in their teaching. In practice, however, several impediments reduced the frequency with which technology got used at the school. Within regular classrooms, a very limited number of computers are available. Best Practice teachers are more supportive than many of having students work on projects in teams, but it is difficult to manage computer-based projects when there are just two or three computers for a class of twenty or twenty-five. Their alternative is scheduling time in the computer lab, but that resource is stretched quite thin. An English teacher expressed this frustration: "If we had the funding to do this, I would love every student to have access to a computer that they could do their drafting on because I think computers are great for revising as you draft."

This same teacher was frustrated also by the lack of keyboarding skills among freshmen. When she did schedule the lab for her students to do word processing, it took longer because of their lack of skill with the keyboard. Moreover, teachers feel that they have to be able to cope with technical as well as content problems to be able to run a class session involving technology. "I actually wish I had more computer training. This thing I'm going to do this summer is take some computer classes because my skills aren't that great either. They're good enough for me to be able to one-on-one tutor somebody, but for me to really run a class with all the different problems that come up on computers, I don't feel like I can handle that."

Technology Plans

Tom Daniels stated his technology infrastructure goal as having four Internet-connected computers in every classroom. (Five or six would be ideal but would not leave enough space for students to sit!) At the time of our case study, most teachers had just one or two computers in their rooms and over a third of these were not Internet connected.

School year 1999–2000 was the first year that Best Practice had a senior class, and the emphasis in assigning resources that year had to be on hiring the six to seven new teachers needed for this class and equipping rooms for them, none of which were wired previously for the LAN. Tom Daniels expected to retire at the end of that year, and he began training math teacher Mark Fertel to take over the technology coordinator role. The school planned also to hire an external consultant to come in and teach HyperStudio, a piece of multimedia development software the staff felt would be a good match to the thematic units and exhibition requirement that are part of the Best Practice approach.

A final technology thrust for 1999–2000 was the ongoing effort to get digital portfolios up and running. Although the staff had talked about them for years, the fact that so much student work had been done off-line made the creation of such portfolios laborious (e.g., work had to be scanned or reentered into a word processing program). Daniels hoped that Open Text Corporation's recent agreement to donate software for creating digital portfolios and to provide teacher training would get the effort off the ground. An added incentive was the desire to give Best Practice seniors an alternative documentation of their accomplishments for use in applying to colleges. The Open Text software also boasts a "collaborative knowledge management system," which Daniels wanted to explore as a support for Best Practice students' collaborative work. "It will be possible for kids while working in groups, for example, on integrated curriculum projects to talk to one another or share their part of it using one of the computers in the cabled room."

Helps and Hindrances Related to the School's Innovative Structure

Although in theory a school oriented around providing opportunities for students to do extended, interdisciplinary projects around authentic tasks should provide extremely fertile ground for technology use, in practice this school faces some barriers that are even more imposing than those in the typical urban high school. Most of these barriers stem not from the Best Practice instructional philosophy but rather from limitations related to the school's small size. Even though the school serves a very high proportion of low-income students, the low total enrollment means that enrollment-based discretionary funding (federal Title I and state Chapter I) is limited. The school has been able to equip only a single modest-sized computer laboratory. Moreover, giving a fair share of time in the computer lab to courses across the curriculum is particularly hard because of the school's block scheduling. Block scheduling, with its longer time periods, is generally regarded as a boon for technology-supported work (Means & Olson, 1994), but it exacerbates the scarcity of technology access in a school with just one computer lab. Teachers who incorporate technology into their hundred-minute block sessions need to book two whole days in the lab if they want to give all of their students a chance for solo use of a computer.

Technical support is limited also; the school's sole on-site technical support is that portion of Tom Daniels's time that is not consumed by other leadership duties. Best Practice has a number of teachers who are adept in using technology, but none of them has the expertise (or the time) to deal with the network. When the LAN goes down, "it's a pain" according to users. During the week of one of our site visits, the network was down and no one had Internet access. Staff had to wait a week for the day that their external consultant spends on-site. Other urban schools serving low-income students are likely to have more funding to work with by virtue of their size and are better able to capitalize on economies of scale in paying for network expenses and technical support.

A second set of challenges stems from the fact that technology is not among the thirteen essential characteristics in the NLU Best Practice model on which the school is based. Technology is viewed as a potential tool for supporting these best practices, but the teachers' prior experience was in schools where technology was available only to students in programming classes and did not support the kind of student-centered, democratic, experiential education that is the top priority at Best Practice. Tom Daniels promoted technology and pushed for devoting a significant portion of staff development time to technology use. Still, it appears that the most active users of technology (e.g., Aiko Boyce and Art Griffin) either had a preexisting involvement with technology or became interested through participation in external teacher networks in their subject areas (e.g., the Hands-On Universe project, the Communication Art Center).

> The biggest issue is to try to get yourself out of the classroom as a teacher to see what else is going on. . . . I really appreciate the experiences that I have had to be a part of several different kinds of programs because you also learn what is going on outside of your own classroom, but also . . . technology and what technology is able to do. You wouldn't learn that if you were always stuck in a class all the time, so you know, having a program like Hands-On Universe to be involved in, Modeling

Physics out of Arizona, the Fermi Lab ARISE Project, all of those have been of great benefit for me personally. . . . Just getting yourself out there, seeing what is out there and learning what technology and new forms of science presentation to the kids that are out there, is really beneficial.

The aversion to teaching skills outside of the context of a broader task that is meaningful to students has led Best Practice to avoid teaching keyboarding and basic computer skills as a separate class. More so than teachers at other case study high schools, Best Practice teachers report feeling hindered in technology use by their students' uneven skill levels.

On the other hand, much about the organization and structure of Best Practice High School makes technology use easier. First, the teachers are highly committed to the school and risk takers by nature. As one Best Practice teacher said, "We're all interested in being on the cutting edge." Best Practice's features of teacher governance and budget flexibility are compatible with supporting teachers who want to acquire technology skills. Tom Daniels noted: "You have to empower teachers. . . . If somebody comes to me and says, 'I need a laptop,' I look for the money."

The school's TRN pointed out that the school was able to hire teachers who hold a similar educational philosophy and believe in the value of technology and that with a staff of just nineteen, it is much easier to bring technology training to everyone. In a small school, ideas spread through informal contacts and through the students. Daniels expressed the hope that the skills students would acquire and the examples of multimedia projects from the studio arts class Aiko Boyce was starting would inspire other teachers to incorporate multimedia projects into their courses.

Issues Shared with Other Schools

While Best Practice's efforts at technology integration are influenced in some ways, both positive and negative, by the school's unique character, they are impacted also by issues shared with other schools. Best Practice teachers tend to be innovative, but they maintain a healthy skepticism toward technology. Art Griffin, for example, notes that implementing technology in the classroom takes time, and teachers should not waste their time or their students' on poor software. Math teacher Mark Fertel feels hampered by the lack of good software for teaching the advanced math skills emphasized in the Best Practice curriculum. He sees most mathematics software as "flash-card-like" drills on basic skills.

The relatively low proportion of software meeting Best Practice teachers' standards adds to the time and effort required to find appropriate materials. Teachers struggle to find time both to educate themselves concerning software options in their fields and then to learn how to actually use the software and incorporate it into their curriculum. Art Griffin comments, "I think that often teachers have a difficult time [not only] trying to keep up with all that technology and the changes that are going on, but then being able to spend the time to learn how to implement it in the curriculum is also difficult."

Griffin makes the point that use of class time is another issue. Many uses of technology, particularly those calling on students to use technology to create products, consume extensive amounts of time. Although proponents of such activities argue that the depth of involvement with a given content area is a strength, teachers, particularly at the high school level, find themselves balancing this claim against pressure to cover a broad curriculum.

> Time is an issue. That is a real issue. Beyond the kids actually creating the project, now they have to take it and put it on the computer, which takes quite a bit of time. And, I will be very honest, there is so much that we are trying to pack into a year's time, that something just has to give in order to accommodate that [technology use], and right now we just have not put a real strong priority to give our kids that kind of time to use HyperStudio, to put together a full presentation. . . . I think [that it is] a very powerful tool, that the kids can actually put

most of what they have learned and accomplished in terms of a finished project in a visual, graphical representation . . . but they have to give up a lot of stuff, in terms of curricular material, to do that.

Implications Regarding the Principal's Role

Our experiences at the two other Chicago high schools, Von Steuben and Bogan, prompted the research team to form the tentative hypothesis that principal leadership is particularly important in bringing technology to urban high schools. In earlier case studies, we have seen elementary schools where a small group of teachers exercised leadership in technology use with principal approval but without strong principal leadership (Means & Olson, 1995). Our visits to technology-using high schools in more affluent suburban communities suggested that technology use there too could be instigated and carried on with only limited principal involvement. At Von Steuben and Bogan, however, it is hard to imagine the kind of technology use they have now without the leadership of their respective principals.

Given Best Practice's alternative structure, what does this case reveal concerning the extent to which we can generalize our premise that principal leadership behind technology use is critical in urban high schools?

At Best Practice, the principal, who is shared with the other multiplex schools, provides administrative management while the lead teachers act as instructional leaders. Principal Sylvia Gibson encourages technology use through example (using technology to communicate with teachers and going through HyperStudio training along with them). At the same time, it is Tom Daniels who articulated an instructional purpose for using technology, made decisions concerning the school's technology infrastructure, arranged technology training for his staff, and solicited external funding to support the school's use of technology, roles played by the principals at the other two Chicago high schools we studied. In addition, unlike the principals, Daniels was actually in the computer lab providing technical support for students and teachers. Thus, Daniels had firsthand knowledge of how Best Practice teachers were using technology with their students.

We do not believe that the Best Practice case provides counterevidence for the proposition that the principal's role is especially critical in technology integration in urban high schools. To the extent that the lead teacher's role differs from that of a principal, it could be argued that the additional authority principals have in terms of staff evaluation and control of resources strengthens their ability to catalyze technology use among their staff. Daniels's decision to set up a single lab with both Macintosh and PC computers, for example, was a compromise that kept all of the teachers happy. Given the additional complications this entailed in terms of keeping the LAN functioning, troubleshooting the computers, and teaching students to use the equipment, it could be argued that a high price was paid for staff consensus.

Strategy for Staff Development

Tom Daniels and the Best Practice teachers think about staff development in much the same way that Richard Gazda and the Von Steuben teachers do. Although there are targeted in-service "show and tells," the main emphasis is on creating a culture of intellectual sharing and an environment in which teachers have the time and space to interact with each other. Clearly Tom and Kathy Daniels have sought to stress these features at their school: "First of all, there has to be an atmosphere of sharing. You have to build in as much common planning time as possible so that this in-servicing can take place, so people can share ideas."

Tom Daniels consciously structured school governance and planning time to provide paid time for Best Practices teachers to collaborate around issues of teaching and learning, including the use of technology. Daniels argued that shared planning time *is* staff development and that teachers should be compensated for this time. "You have got to have the common planning done. Build in as much as you can. We pay our teachers as much as we can. If they stay after school, we put that in the budget because we think that they are professionals. . . . Common planning time is staff development. It is all part of the same thing."

Although Daniels used common planning time for staff meetings incorporating informal in-service training, many of the Best Practice teachers stressed the importance of having more individualized and extended teacher learning opportunities as well. When asked how teachers can acquire skill in using technology in their teaching, Aiko Boyce sounds much like Von Steuben's Lucja Kowalski. The two are similar in their pessimism over prospects for group workshops on technology to help teachers really change their practice. Like Kowalski, Boyce advocates one-on-one collaborations and opportunities to observe other teachers using technology with students.

> I guess I feel that in order to make a real impression . . . [schools must] create a situation where at least both of our classes would be covered, and then I could work with that person almost one on one. I really feel that will work. I don't really know about more than one on one. Maybe one on three, but then you know, logistically you are having the problem of where are these people going to be and how are you going to cover them. But we need something . . . really close so that they [the learning teachers] feel they have got someone they can kind of bond with, you know, and maybe larger teacher workshops are feasible, but to me, I often wonder how serious those people are who take those teacher workshops, really. When I am working with you one on one, and I know you've got questions, that is going to tell me whether you are really interested or not. . . . It might not be the most efficient way, one might say, because you are not hitting three hundred teachers at one time, but if you took one or two teachers that are going to make any kind of impact,

the impact is going to come from showing it to their classes and then from there it will kind of ignite and spread out.

Another important aspect of Best Practice's approach toward teacher learning is the stress on giving teachers decision-making power. Daniels explained, "Once you get the common planning time, they decide. Sometimes I will say I am bringing in a speaker . . . we got this new gift and you have to know how to work it. . . . Other times they will say, 'Listen, we want to know how to do this.' Okay, we will set aside two hours and do that. So they have a great deal of say so. That is part of their empowerment."

Tom Daniels described teacher empowerment with respect to their own learning as critical to making a school work. Looking forward to retirement, Tom and Kathy Daniels realized that the course of the school and its use of technology would depend on the quality of the new leadership.[1] The Danielses expressed confidence that the shared leadership model has given Best Practice teachers the understanding and the will to continue in the same mold. Said Tom, "If you're going to go out, this is the way to do it. These teachers will carry it on."

---

[1] During the two years of our case study, Tom Daniels was battling cancer. He died in November 1999, and we dedicate this chapter to his memory with gratitude and respect for his unflagging dedication to making urban schools a positive force in the lives of students.

6

Taking It to the Next Level

SEEKING TECHNOLOGY
TO MATCH THEIR STUDENTS

"You don't want to trap the pictures," says Amika, a senior at Renaissance High School in Detroit, explaining how text and pictures are laid out in two pages of the school yearbook. Pointing to the computer screen, Amika goes on to explain that it's good to make sure "you break the eye line" by spreading pictures across two pages of the yearbook, thus "crossing the gutter." The program Amika and her classmates were using, called Elite Vision (beta version), was making it possible for Renaissance students to create and edit their yearbook on computers at the school for the first time.

When asked where she learned the design principles behind laying out the yearbook, Amika was quick to point out that her teacher, Ramonda Hollenquest, taught her much of what she knows in class. But Amika learned many things simply through the experience of using Elite Vision. She could explain how to modify each page layout, change views, and move pages from one section to another, and she could relate the computer program's visual tools to traditional processes of laying out a newspaper or yearbook using paper and ink. "These blue lines on the screen," she explains, "are like the columns on graph paper that we use to lay the paper out by hand. Having lots of lines on the screen frees you up to have lots of different column sizes." As she talks, Amika points to the lines on the screen and demonstrates several different column widths across different pages of the yearbook.

The school almost did not get the software that Amika has become so skillful in using and demonstrating, though. According to Hollenquest, the company could only make the donation to one high school, and Renaissance was in competition with suburban West Bloomfield High School (described in Chapter Eight) for the software. Although the company wanted to support the urban school, Hollenquest's classrooms had no computers that could run the software. The school would have to come up with at least six new computers before the start of the school year to run the program.

The school's principal, Dr. Irma Hamilton, told district technology officials of the story and invited them to see firsthand how little technology Renaissance had at the school. In part as a result of the visit, the school was granted twenty-five new computers, six of which went to Hollenquest's room, thus ensuring that Renaissance would be able to receive the Elite Vision program for the yearbook. The editing of the yearbook, once a painstaking process over which students and the school had little control, has become much more something that Amika and the other students in Hollenquest's yearbook class could design and manage themselves. Acquiring this new software, though, was a small victory in what has been a long and difficult struggle for Renaissance to secure technology access for its students. Only in the 2000–01 school year, after the period of our fieldwork, has this struggle begun to pay off, as new wireless laptops with advanced multimedia capabilities and a new technology coordinator brightened the school's prospects for creating a technology-rich school. As Hamilton notes, "Where we were is not where we are now. We're in a position to give students good exposure to technology."

"Academics First": A Detroit Magnet with Expectations for Excellence

Renaissance High School is one of three selective magnet schools in the Detroit Public Schools (DPS). Renaissance and its two counterparts, Cass Technical High School and Martin Luther King High School, compete for Detroit's most academically talented students each year. Renaissance has always been quite successful in luring top students, even when its facilities and access to technology were limited. An estimated third of the school's entering freshmen come from private or parochial middle schools, simply to attend what they see as the premier school in the city.

Students from the highest achievement levels often choose to attend Renaissance because of its small size and its reputation for academic excellence, which extends well beyond Detroit itself. With 860 students, Renaissance is the smallest of Detroit's public high schools. The ethnic composition of the school is similar to that of other schools in the district (nearly 100 percent African American), but parents are atypical in terms of education and occupations. Administrators report that the majority of Renaissance's students' parents are middle-class professionals and community leaders who have high expectations for their children's academic success. In 1998 *U.S. News & World Report* recognized Renaissance as one of the top one hundred public schools in America, citing its academic focus and expectations for excellence as distinguishing features of the school.

Once admitted to Renaissance, students must work hard to succeed and to contribute to the school's overall record of accomplishments. The school requires all students to maintain a 2.5 GPA, and to keep their grades up, students must be self-motivated. Few external academic supports are available for struggling students, and teachers, peers, and parents all maintain high expectations for academic excellence. Teachers at Renaissance give challenging assignments to students and expect them to master a rigorous college-preparatory curriculum that includes four years of English, mathematics, science, social studies, and foreign language. Students, for their part, keep meticulous track of their grades, and at the end of each marking period, disappointed students can be found standing in line before teachers' offices to see what they can do to raise their grades. Parents are especially involved in setting these expectations. They come often to parent-teacher conferences, raise funds through the PTA and various booster clubs, and have their own orientation when their children enter ninth grade. The whole school community seems committed to the school's slogan, "Academics First."

The competitive atmosphere extends beyond the school walls. Students from Renaissance regularly compete in local, state, and national academic competitions. One group of students won second place in the National Quiz Bowl competition in San Diego in 1998. That same year, two of the school's students won first and second place in the Wayne State University Quiz Bowl. Students from Renaissance won the Grand Award, first, second, and third place awards in the Detroit Metropolitan Science Fair. In the 2000–01 year, there are plans to create a special class for students who plan to compete in the national academic decathlon.

The school's success is not limited to traditional academics. Two students were recently selected to become a part of the Alvin Ailey American Dance Center. In the State Solo Ensemble Festival, Renaissance students won "superior" and "excellent" ratings. In 1999 they were the U.S. Chess Federation High School Champions. In 1999–2000, the school's men's basketball team won the city championship against several larger schools and went to the state quarterfinals for its division. The school points with pride to three former Renaissance football players who are on academic-athletic scholarships at Duke University.

For their efforts, Renaissance students have been recognized and rewarded when they apply for admission into four-year colleges and universities. According to one of the school's college counselors, 100 percent of seniors are accepted into a four-year college or university. In 1998–99 there were twelve National Merit finalists, ninety Michigan Competitive Scholarship semifinalists, and forty-eight Superintendent's Banquet awardees. Some 4.7 million dollars in scholarships and grants were awarded to college-bound Renaissance seniors. Many colleges, aware of the caliber of Renaissance's students, moreover, come to Renaissance and admit students on the spot, once they've seen their academic and extracurricular records. One student SRI researchers interviewed said he'd just chosen to go to Florida A&M. When asked how he decided, he said the university had come to

Renaissance to recruit and promised a full, four-year scholarship for students willing to go into the sciences and engineering. He applied and was admitted with a full scholarship with a declared major of computer engineering.

A School Struggling to Provide Technology Access

In 1998 Renaissance developed an ambitious technology plan, calling for 450 to 600 networked workstations, each with a high-bandwidth connection to the Internet. Each department formulated its own plan for how those computers would be used:

- The Business and Accounting Department would use computers to support a program that allows students to invest money in the stock market and a new school-to-career program.

- Counseling and Guidance would use the Internet to research colleges and universities, search for scholarships, and apply to college and for financial aid.

- The English Department would use the Internet to conduct research, communicate with students from other countries, and support student literary Web pages, among other plans.

- The Fine Arts Department would be able to access and listen to choral performances and to use CD-ROMs to provide context to dance and movement classes.

- Foreign Language would like to use laser disk, video, and audio technology to provide enhanced opportunities for students to practice learning a second language.

- The Library would like to transform itself into a full-service library media center.

- The Mathematics Department would like to incorporate more calculator-based laboratories and multimedia design tools to support mathematical concept development.

- The Science Department would like to use the Internet to connect students to scientists.

- Social Studies would like to use the Internet to conduct research using this "global library" to investigate issues such as the role of demographics in public policy and global warming.

Despite its vision, high academic standards, and reputation, at the time of our case study Renaissance High School was struggling to find enough computer technology to implement its technology plan and support students' interests and desire to use new technologies in their classes. Like other urban high schools, Renaissance is faced with limited budgets and the need to form partnerships with businesses and community groups to acquire technology. Because Renaissance students are economically advantaged by DPS standards (only 16 percent of students on free or reduced-price lunch) and because the school has had difficulties negotiating relationships with business partners, at the time of our study Renaissance had obtained little in the way of technology funding or donations. As a result, Renaissance had far fewer computers than schools such as Murray-Wright, and students' Internet access was limited to a few computers in one room within the school. As Dr. Hamilton explains, "Our funds have to come to us from some other means, like grants or companies that try to adopt [us], but unfortunately some of the stuff that they have given us is old. They may refurbish it, but it's not the kind of equipment that we need to really push our students forward."

Miriam Turner, the Science Department chair, adds, "We've been trying to get donations from everybody. . . . I guess it's because our scores are so high [they think] that we don't need anything. That is so wrong."

Even when the school does acquire equipment, it faces additional problems in trying to maintain equipment and help teachers learn how to use new technologies. Many at the school believe that these elements should be regular line items in the school budget.

According to one teacher:

> I think that anytime that new technology is brought into the
> school, it's just like the maintenance should be built into the
> budget. Also built into the budget should be servicing. . . . I take
> classes every summer for whatever is coming up in the fall. It
> should be a part of the program. We should have professionals
> come in and not only teach us . . . on the minimum entry level
> but maybe beyond—at least in-service for the teachers.

As recently as the 1999–2000 school year, only five rooms in the
school had computers for student use. The first computer lab established at Renaissance, originally called the "Center for Enhanced
Instruction" and now known as the "FAMS Lab," is on the third
floor. At any one time the lab has held between ten and twenty of
the school's newer IBM Windows-based computers, nine of which
were currently connected to the Internet at the time of our study.
One lab of thirty-six IBM Windows-based computers is used for the
district-required Computer Applications classes, taught by Lilly Gladney. The room where students take journalism and yearbook houses
six computers, and the library has five Dell computers. In 1999–2000
only the library computers and three computers in the counseling
office were available for drop-in use, leaving students to compete for
scarce technology resources for completing any out-of-class assignments that require them to use computers. Kinko's was mentioned by
several students as a likely place to find Renaissance students when
such assignments are due.

Starting with Less

With just 16 percent of students eligible for free or subsidized lunches,
the Renaissance High School student body has fewer low-income
students than most other Detroit public high schools. As a result,
Renaissance winds up with fewer discretionary funds to spend on
technology than most other high schools in Detroit, precisely

because the school has more advantaged students than its counterparts in the inner city. Schools like Murray-Wright receive extensive federal Title I and state 31A compensatory education funding to address the academic needs of low-income students. Many schools use compensatory education funds to buy computers, technical support, and professional development time for teachers to learn how to use new technologies. This approach works particularly well in districts like DPS that encourage schoolwide Title I programs. These same schools also receive higher proportions of federal E-rate funding, allowing them to get subsidies to help connect schools to the Internet. Schools with more advantaged students get fewer, less significant, subsidies (if any) when it comes to wiring and networking computers to the Web.

Because of the way DPS allocates Title I funds, Renaissance receives a minimal amount of discretionary funding each year (e.g., in 2000–01, the school received no Title I money, compared with $208,604 for Murray-Wright). In the absence of extraordinary steps to make room for technology in the school budget or successful efforts to bring in additional funds through winning grants for the introduction of technology, there are no technology funds for schools like Renaissance. As a result, the school has far fewer computers than most other Detroit high schools, limited technical support secured from outside vendors, and only a few computers connected to the Internet. The technology Renaissance does have can be traced to the actions of parent groups, business partners, and the actions of individual district administrators responding to extreme needs. Parent groups, moreover, are often called on to address competing school needs, including support for the school's facilities and sports teams.

When working with any outside partners, the school must often answer questions brought about by its own success. Renaissance students seem to do well on their own, without the benefit of using new technologies. The core curriculum emphasizes important critical thinking skills embedded within traditional disciplines and prepares students for admission into some of the state's and nation's most competitive four-year colleges. The students, moreover, come from more-advantaged backgrounds than many of their peers attending other Detroit public high schools. Renaissance teachers say that outsiders familiar with the advantages Renaissance students already enjoy ask tough questions when asked to support the school's technology initiative: Why does Renaissance need new technologies? Shouldn't other, more-disadvantaged students get new technologies to help them get a leg up? Why mess with the traditional pencil-and-paper-based curriculum, if it works?

Critics of educational technology like Cuban (1986) have raised similar questions about schools' investments in new technologies. They argue that the money being spent on technology would better be spent preparing teachers to help students learn higher-order thinking skills in a college-preparatory curriculum similar to the one that Renaissance currently offers. But the reactions of business-people and district officials who have visited the school and seen how limited the technology resources there are suggest that there may be another important reason why students at a school like Renaissance need more technology access—to give some of the city's most talented minority students the chance to go even further by giving them experience with the kinds of tools they will use in higher education and eventually in the workplace.

Renaissance's Business Partnerships: Frustrated Expectations

When Lear Corporation executives from Southfield, Michigan, first visited Renaissance, they saw a tremendous opportunity. Here was a bright and responsible group of students who might one day work for Lear, one of the world's largest auto suppliers. Providing technology to the school would not only encourage these youth to consider working for Lear after college but also would contribute to Lear's growing reputation as a good corporate citizen. Lear has been involved in a number of philanthropic and social justice efforts aimed at increasing economic opportunities for African Americans. It has given to other education initiatives and was the major contributor to the career center at Michigan State University in East Lansing. In 1997 Lear was awarded the Ford Motor Company Corporate Citizen Award for leading in buying goods and materials from minority-owned companies(The Auto Channel, 1997).

Renaissance mathematics department chair Phil Lampi, who acted as the technology liaison for the school until his retirement in 2000, had been active in trying to build partnerships with area businesses like Lear ever since he became the school's point man for technology. Lear's visit in 1998 resulted in what Lampi construed as a promise of some one hundred desktop computers, to be delivered over the summer. Lear was particularly interested in supporting the school's new Ford Academy of Manufacturing Science (FAMS) program, a parallel program to the one at Murray-Wright. The main goal of the program is consistent with Lear's own corporate interests in giving to the school: to prepare students for the twenty-first-century workplace, which includes technology tools. The program introduces students to careers in manufacturing and manufacturing technology and includes teaching interviewing skills, field trips to businesses, and high-paying summer jobs ($14/hour). In exchange for donating one hundred computers, Lear wanted to be given the first slot in interviewing potential interns from Renaissance, a condition to which Lampi reluctantly agreed.

Lampi and other faculty at the school were disappointed when the computers did not arrive in time for the start of school year 1998–99. Rooms had been prepared for the computers' arrival, but none arrived by fall of 1998. Then in the fall of 1999 Lear sent the school just twenty-five of the promised computers. These computers all had between 16 and 25 MB of RAM, and none was new or powerful enough to run many of the programs that the school had purchased for its computer classes in Web page design and desktop publishing. Many sat unplugged in the FAMS lab room awaiting upgrades promised by the district before they were dispersed across the school. Later the twenty-five new computers paid for through district funds arrived, and most of the Lear computers were removed from the lab altogether. According to Lampi, getting older computers like the ones Lear gave is a mixed blessing for the school, if a blessing at all: "They've created more problems than what it was worth. Some got used a little bit for word processing, but not much else."

In spring of 1999 Sequoia Corporation, a Michigan-based company that provides integration and administration services for Windows NT-based environments to companies, made a visit to Renaissance with some officials from Lear. The company representatives were dismayed that the school had such limited technology resources. The Sequoia representatives said that they would hire a number of students as interns in network design, noting the high quality of Renaissance students. In the end, none of the students was hired, and none of the students was notified by the company that they did not get the internships. Lampi reports that Sequoia also promised to install a new lab in the school, but a year later, nothing had been done. Sequoia has been building a lab for Detroit Country Day School, a nearby private school, and had been given a number of free laptops by Dell, from whom they had purchased computers for Country Day. Sequoia promised Renaissance some of these laptops and an opportunity to partner with Country Day to develop a technology-integrated curriculum, but to date Renaissance has not received any of the computers and has not been involved in the curriculum development projects at all.

Some of these disappointments are probably endemic to school-business partnerships and not at all specific to Renaissance. Company management turns over, and yesterday's plan is always subject to a reversal from the new decision maker. Moreover, individual corporate visitors to Renaissance, struck as we were by the mismatch between the high level of student and teacher excellence and the inadequacy of their technology supports, may be tempted to think out loud about supports they would like to provide but may not have authority to commit. It is likely also that nothing in the training or prior experience of school staff has prepared them to be "deal closers" and to implement strategies to get corporate benefactors to make firm, clear commitments that are more difficult to reverse.

Not all of Renaissance's partnerships with local businesses have been as problematic and disappointing as the ones just described. An example of a small but successful partnership is one with Capital Management Corporation, which gave $10,000 in real money to AP Economics students to invest in the stock market. In addition, many cooperative arrangements allow Renaissance students to go to corporate sites to access technology. For example, journalism students can help design and lay out their school newspaper at the Detroit *Free Press* offices, which is helpful because they cannot do full layouts of their paper at school. In addition, a number of art students have participated in the SCOOP program at Wayne State, in which students use video editing equipment to edit their own videos. Others have gone to programs at a city art school that teaches how to create animated videos. Recently, Renaissance students did a tribute piece on Gordon Parks that was shown at the Detroit Art Institute.

The disappointments encountered in the more ambitious business partnerships that were expected to bring significantly more technology into the school have decreased morale and lowered expectations among those teachers who most want to use technology, especially among those involved in forming and maintaining these partnerships. Still, Renaissance has few other options than to attempt to maintain good relationships with business partners like Lear and Sequoia if they are to improve technology access for their students significantly in the coming years. There are no other large sources of funding or giving for the school to court, and district funds are limited. The district itself is also a player in these business partnerships, and to succeed in implementing its ambitious technology plan, Renaissance must work carefully and collaboratively with DPS to ensure that they have technical support for the hardware that business partners promise to provide.

Working with the District to Acquire New Technology

District officials who have visited the school have had similar responses to the relative absence of computer technology at Renaissance. They are puzzled that the school has little technology, and have sought to help address the problem. Recently, the district's chief information officer toured the school and asked, "Where are the computers?" His surprise at the lack of technology at Renaissance led him to send twenty-five new IBM computers the next day (the computers now in the FAMS lab and Hollenquest's room).

This recent case of rapid, tangible district support stands in contrast to some past actions, which some school staff members interpreted as district interference. Several years ago Lampi had secured an agreement with a company called SpeedChoice to install an innovative wireless T-1 connection to the school. The school would use the company's own network and was promised a high-speed, high-bandwidth connection to the Internet. The district's information systems management director vetoed the plan, however. According to Lampi, the district has attempted to block purchases of computers as well, in some cases deeming the Math Department head's choices as "too powerful for the school's needs." At one time, district staff decided not to support a set of Pentium II computers Lampi wanted to purchase at discount from a business partner. District staff reasoned that they would not be able to provide technical support to the machines if they broke down.

Although helpful, onetime equipment allocations from sympathetic district administrators who happen to visit the school are an inadequate basis for integrating technology throughout the curriculum. Only recently has the district become more involved in helping to wire Renaissance for the Internet, supporting a school partnership with Sequoia to provide a new backbone for the building. Renaissance finds itself in the same position with the district, however, as it does with its business partners. Without a regular budget for purchasing and supporting enough new technology to implement fully the school's technology plan, the school has no choice but to depend on its own entrepreneurial efforts to persuade district officials to help Renaissance reach its goals. It is hard to argue with the Renaissance teacher who described the resulting process as "piecemeal."

To be sure, the district has laid important groundwork for making technology much more a part of the core curriculum. According to Juanita Clay-Chambers, the associate superintendent for educational services, each curriculum area at every grade level now has technology standards built into the curriculum. Renaissance will soon benefit from this integration at some level, when AP Statistics students receive some 105 new graphing calculators that are a part of a new district textbook adoption plan. But other academic departments are still far from equipped to take advantage of technology in their subject areas.

Technology in the College-Preparatory Curriculum: Enhancing Conceptual Understanding

Although Renaissance has lacked a good technology infrastructure, it does have a key ingredient for effective technology use. The school's teachers are confident in their command of their subject matter and accustomed to leading their students through inquiry-based learning.

This facility shows in the way math teacher Joe Bell uses graphing calculators, handheld computing devices that are already a significant part of Renaissance students' mathematics experience. Although there are no desktop computers in the mathematics classrooms, several teachers use graphing calculators regularly, in an effort to help enhance students' understanding of math concepts through visualization. According to students in Bell's Precalculus class, for example, "We use the calculators pretty much every day."

Bell's Precalculus class consists mostly of eleventh and twelfth graders, all of whom are college-bound. The younger students in the class are all ranked close to the top of their classes and are seeking admission to very competitive colleges. The room is set up into six clusters of four tables where students are seated in small groups. At the front of the room is a chalkboard. There is one Power Macintosh in the back of the room for the teacher's use. On the day we observed Bell's class, students were all using TI-83 calculators to solve an extra credit problem involving slant asymptotes.

Bell explained that the problem involved synthetic division, and asked, "How many people like synthetic division?" Three students raised their hand. "Because a lot of people like synthetic division a whole lot," added Bell. Next he asked, "How many people know what an asymptote is?" Students clearly had some exposure to the idea of asymptotes. Bell asked a student who raised her hand to describe in her own words what an asymptote is.

"Where the solutions to the thing approach a certain number," she replied.

"Solutions to the . . . FUNCTION," corrected Bell. "Who can say more?"

"It seems to go to zero or something," added another student.

"Is it ever going to get there?" Bell asked. He then introduced the notion of a limit and numbers approaching asymptotes in a function. Aware that this was a new concept for many of the students, "Have we talked about limits?" He described limits as "end behaviors" of a graph. He described a function where the value oscillates around its limit as an example of an asymptote (a possible counterexample to the idea that a function never has the value of its limit).

As we watched, Bell explained they will graph an equation with a slant asymptote. He had the students get out their calculators and enter the equation:

$$y = (8x^2 - 4x + 11)/(x + 11)$$

He asked the students to do a "ZoomFit" to expand the view of the graph, so that all values of the function could be seen on their screens.

Students passed around graphing calculators to each other to verify. Bell encouraged students to work together to solve the problem. For the most part, all the students were on task. In one group of tables, students were talking among themselves because they had different views of the graph, and they called Bell over to take a look. One student had a view showing a parabola with no slant asymptote at all.

After going to several tables, Bell discovered that most students were having trouble with their graphs. Only one student had created a graph that represented the slant asymptote function correctly. Bell noted that in the previous class, they'd had no trouble getting the functions to graph correctly. He said, "Go to Windows, and set the following parameters:

Put X minimum = − 50

X maximum =+50

X scl =1

Y minimum = − 340

Y maximum =140

This time, all the students got the correct graphs, and Bell called a young woman up to the board to perform synthetic division to find the equation of the asymptote. She got nearly through but got stuck trying to figure out what to do with the remainder. Bell asked if anyone could help her. One student volunteered to tell her how to do it, but Bell suggested, "Why don't you go up yourself and do your own explanation. It's kind of like putting people on the spot to have to tell them what to do like that." At this point, Bell gave students the answer to the problem and asked them about the plausibility of the equation. "Could −44 be the y-intercept?" he asked. A student replied, "Yes, because we set the scale so big." (The representation on the board showed the y-intercept close to 0.) "Is the slope +8 reasonable?" "Yes, because it's positive."

Using technology like graphing calculators, according to Bell, helps students understand the "big ideas" of the mathematics he is teaching. He believes calculators are helpful because the "numbers get in the way" of students getting these big ideas sometimes. Technology allows students to discern patterns, sequences, and limits, for example, by seeing instantly how an equation is an exemplar of an asymptotic function. In the class we observed, Bell asked students to think about the "plausibility" of the equation, not just generate the right answer, and he was able to focus on the reasons students gave for their answers.

Technology, then, allows Bell to have students do more problem solving. The mechanics of doing calculations are taken care of, so students can focus more on the mental processes in solving a problem. This is especially important for helping students be prepared to do well on the tests that are part of the Michigan Educational Assessment Program, he believes, where mathematical problem solving is emphasized.

Bell is not the only Renaissance teacher who uses technology to enhance students' conceptual understanding of difficult subject matter. AP Economics teacher Gary Hudkins uses simulations of supply and demand on CD-ROMs that come with the AP Economics textbook and has students research stock prices on the Internet to teach principles of markets. Hudkins's AP class participated in the stock market investment project with funds provided by Capital Management Corporation. Students got a classwide Internet account with Charles Schwab, investigated stock prices and price:earnings ratios, and made a 10 percent return on the $10,000 that Capital Management gave them to invest. As participants in the experience, students got to keep 25 percent of the profits they earned.

Science teachers under the leadership of department head Miriam Turner participate in computer-based investigations that involve students in learning through simulations and field-based inquiry. In the BioBlast program, for example, students use calculator-based labs to model lunar environments under constraints discovered by NASA's Advanced Life Support Research. In the

EPA-funded and Wayne County–managed Rouge River Project, Renaissance students participate along with other high school students from across the Detroit Metro area in tracking the water quality of the Rouge River, a tributary that feeds into the Detroit River. Some forty schools participate in the project, taking measurements of nine dimensions of water quality, including water temperature, pH, alkalinity, nitrates, and dissolved oxygen. The data are used to inform researchers at SIMCOG, a local policy group focused on environmental conservation issues. In the month leading up to the data collection day, Turner teaches students about key concepts involved in the measure of water quality. She has students review past data since the project began in 1989, both from Renaissance and from other schools along the river. Because of the inadequacy of the Internet access at their school, students enter their water quality data on the Internet at home and then analyze annual progress in the improvement of the Rouge River's water quality.

In both the economics project and the Rouge River project, computers play an important role, but they are hardly ubiquitous in the classroom. Hudkins had students use the two computers and dial-up modem in the Social Studies office to do their research, and his ability to use the simulations on the CD-ROM in his teaching was limited to what he could show when he moved these computers into his classroom for the day. Turner, similarly, had to collect computers from around the school and cart them to her class to carry out the Rouge River project. The students do not enter Renaissance's data at school, since many have faster, more reliable connections to the Internet at home. Although both these projects invite students to use technology to enhance their understanding of difficult subject matter, in the end the role of technology is undermined by the lack of access, even though both teachers report that the technological aspects of the projects are particularly interesting and engaging. Without greater technology access in regular classrooms at Renaissance, only a few teachers even attempt to involve their students in such technology-supported projects.

A New Arena for Excellence: Students Creating Computer Art

Oni Akilah is a thirty-year veteran teacher, who has been at Renaissance since near the beginning of the school's history in 1980. Before coming to Renaissance, she was an art teacher at the elementary level. She has taught freehand drawing, painting, calligraphy, and computer art at Renaissance. She has been using technology for approximately three years, beginning with taking a keyboarding class at Randolph Vocational Center. She first integrated technology into her calligraphy class, and last year she was approached by the administration to offer a computer art class.

Developing Students' Images of "Wilderness"

In late fall, students in Akilah's class began exploring Photoshop by using images found in the "Wilderness" folder that comes with the software. On the day we visited, students were experimenting with the process of cloning, or copying, an image and combining this task with using other tools of Adobe Photoshop they had already learned. The students were in the early phases of learning how to use the tool, and on this particular day, they were using an image of the skull of a steer hanging on a wooden fence. Students were supposed to cut out the image of the skull itself and use the cloning function to create an original design with the skull, creating a single design by the end of the class period.

This activity was intended to lead up to what Akilah describes as a "best design," which would incorporate students' own images and demonstrate their skill in using the Photoshop functions they had learned so far into an integrated design. Later, students scanned five photographs of themselves and five photographs of different kinds of environments and were asked to use the vertical and filtering tools to create their own representation of the concept of "wilderness."

From late winter to early spring, the students' work progressed significantly. When we returned in April, each student had completed and matted both a self-portrait and a piece that represented "wilderness." They had used both the vertical and filtering tools in producing their pieces. Akilah had entered nine of the pieces in the Detroit Institute for the Arts annual student art competition, and one student's self-portrait, depicting four layers of identity (including his membership in JROTC), won an award. A second student won an award for a documentary video about a trip that thirty-three history, English, and art students from Renaissance had taken to retrace the march from Selma to Montgomery. A part of this video aired on Black Entertainment Television in the summer of 2000.

Akilah commented that what the technology allowed students to do is to create more-sophisticated works of art as they learned how to combine different tools. At first, when they were using only the vertical tools, students' images were fairly simple, but with each assignment, Akilah says she saw a "big jump" in the quality of student work. For their final project, she had students do three "final" versions of projects, by having them complete a draft, scan it, and "take it to the next level" three different times.

The transformations in student work were indeed quite dramatic. In the fall, students' designs were fairly simple and abstract. The designs did not show much evidence of the use of design principles (e.g., composition, contrast, use of color) but reflected students' own individualistic styles. Text was used in many of the designs, and in one case was quite creative. A student had taken three images of the steer skull and posed the question "Do you still want that burger?" (Asked if he was a vegetarian, he replied "no," but he certainly appeared ripe for conversion.)

By spring, students' images were far more sophisticated compositions. Students had all scanned in images of themselves, of places in their neighborhood, and objects of personal value; many had drawn original images to include in their compositions. Both the "Wilderness" and "Self-Portrait" compositions were intricately organized and used color in appealing ways, demonstrating students' skill in applying the technical tools of Photoshop to a particular artistic problem.

Transforming the Teaching of Art

Akilah says that she had taught painting and drawing so long that she had developed a set way of teaching. With the new Computer Art class, she reports feeling more open; she feels more free to act as a facilitator. She says it is good to watch students figure out how to solve problems on their own. As advice to other teachers implementing technology in art for the first time, Akilah suggested, "Let the students teach you."

Indeed, an observer to the class would find that most of the students work comfortably on their own, with little assistance from Akilah, even though her high standards for their work are apparent when students explain what they are doing. Students rely extensively on peer help to learn how to perform specific software commands. For example, one girl called for help to a nearby senior who was quite skilled in using Photoshop. She asked her to help with cutting out the image of the steer skull and pasting it into a new sheet. The more expert student helped the first student accomplish this and showed her how to "clean up" the image by using the lasso tool to cut away the shadows at the edge of the skull. In the process, the senior also demonstrated how to change the View (by zooming in) to make the task easier.

Akilah is comfortable working both one step ahead and one step behind her students. She often refers to a list of software functions and commands she keeps on a notepad when students have questions. Sometimes another one of her students will suggest a solution to a problem a fellow student is having, and Akilah is comfortable with students being the experts. At one point in a class we observed, for example, a student was having trouble using the cloning tool in Photoshop. She had created a single image, with conical shapes in the background and the text "Life Over Death" centered on the screen. Akilah was having trouble with cloning as well and turned to her notepad with tips on it for using particular functions. When these failed, she tried herself, but to no avail. She asked a nearby student for help. The student tried to solve the problem and was similarly unsuccessful, but he was able to come up with a way to work around it.

Learning how to use the software tools is just one goal of the Computer Art class. Akilah is most interested in helping students learn the basics and intricacies of artistic design. Over the course of two semesters, students learn the basics of the software and gain practice in the tool using existing photos, scanning in original photos they have taken, and integrating design with expression of their own identities. Along the way, Akilah teaches key concepts of design, including composition, color theory, positive and negative space, texture, and linear design. Akilah observes that the students who have taken her Foundations class or who have a strong background in the arts seem to excel the most in this new medium. Still, Akilah argues that those students who would not be drawn to art necessarily are engaged by using Photoshop. The pace for students with less initial interest in art is more accelerated than it otherwise would be—due largely to the students' comfort with technology. Akilah says, "It allows people to see that art is really everything."

A Future for Computer Art at Renaissance?
Providing Desktop Publishing Services for the School

Like other teachers seeking to teach with technology at Renaissance, Akilah faces the problem of limited access. There were only ten available computers with the Photoshop software, and all were located on the third floor in the school's FAMS lab. The one printer and scanner were both down in the basement. Akilah had hoped to introduce Adobe Illustrator to the students as well, but the software did not come in at all. "If I had had enough computers, we could have moved twice as fast," Akilah reflects. "We're doing the same things I had planned to do, just doing it at a slow pace with students getting to the computers every three days." The students learned the technical skills quickly, but with only a few computers and programs, Akilah says she was unable to keep pace with the students' desire to learn and produce. In an attempt to address this problem, Akilah plans to provide a service to the school that could help raise money for new computers. Upon completion of their self-portraits and wilderness compositions, students were beginning a new project, producing brochures for each department for Renaissance's spring Open House. Students were to collect information and pictures from each department to include in the brochure, and Akilah planned to use the project to teach students desktop publishing. Some software was installed already on FAMS machines, and Akilah saw the project as an opportunity to meet two goals: to teach students skills in designing brochures and to help make the case schoolwide for the need for new computers for her classes.

Akilah comments that while her students have a basic familiarity and comfort with technology stemming from exposure at home, there are major gaps in their technology skills. "They're very comfortable using the tool, [but they're] not as knowledgeable as you assume." Her understanding echoed what students told us: if they have the software at home, they rarely use it for the purposes that Akilah has them using it for at school. When she had students begin to learn Announcement 7.0 (a desktop publishing program) and PageMaker to develop a brochure and business card, she had expected the project to be a review. But none of the students had done a brochure before, and many of the brochures reflected the fact that if students had ever done any desktop publishing before, they had not mastered either kerning (adjusting the space between letters) or leading (adjusting the space between lines of text). Many of their fonts crowded on the page when printed. Akilah hoped the departmental brochure project would help students hone these skills and learn to produce more elegant brochure designs.

Students: Using Technology Wherever They Can

Like their teachers, Renaissance students are a resourceful lot. Although there are not enough computers in classrooms to integrate technology throughout the curriculum, students still manage to find ways to use technology to do their work and to exercise their creativity. The lack of technology, moreover, does not appear to deflect them from considering careers in the sciences, engineering, and the high-tech industry. Nevertheless, these Detroit students of color, many of whom will go to elite, predominantly white institutions of higher education, will face competition from students who have had technology integrated into their math and science courses from middle school on. According to Lawrence Snyder, professor of computer science at the University of Washington who chaired the National Research Council committee issuing its report on information technology skills required for the workplace (National Research Council, 1999), college is "too late" to begin the process of developing fluency with information technology (Snyder, 2000).

Students with Commitment and Initiative

The Renaissance student body is composed of young men and women of unusual initiative and drive to succeed. They take pride and responsibility in maintaining the school and its reputation as a center of academic excellence. Many students are active on the local school site council, in sports, in extracurricular activities, and in forming their own organizations to support the school. When students perceive problems in the school, they take action to remedy them. The "Men of Vision," for example, is a group that started when students perceived a behavior problem within the school. These students function as role models and as tutors for other students and have become a key group in maintaining the culture of the school.

Even if technology is not readily available, Renaissance students will occasionally bring it to school from home or go out of their way to borrow what limited equipment there is to complete a project. SRI researchers followed one junior who was walking through the hallways with a digital camera. The camera was recording his movements as he walked down the hall. We caught up to him in the Renaissance gym, where he explained that he was making a "Day in the Life" kind of video, a project for a class he was taking, with a video camera he had brought from home. Determined to make his video, this student was simply making do with what he had, something that other students seemed accustomed to doing as well. Students are well aware that there are few places for them to use technology in the school. According to one girl, "We need some printers in this school. They need to update all the programs. We've got programs from like 1770 here, no Internet access, and no scanners."

Not having enough computers, printers, and Internet connections does not seem to stop Renaissance students: there are numerous examples of student work on the walls of the school showing computer-generated art, research papers, and even a student-designed Web page for the JROTC program. (http://hometown.aol.com/rotc221155/index.html).

Working with the Pressure to Succeed

Renaissance teachers know that their students can be expected to find a way to accomplish something, even if they encounter many obstacles. Teachers themselves use the computers in the departmental office to maintain grades on spreadsheets and other grading programs, but they are not the only ones who use these computers. Students may be found using these computers when teachers are not. While SRI researchers were interviewing Miriam Turner, for example, two students were busy working on a paper using the science department offices. They and other students told us that many teachers routinely give assignments that require them to use a word processor to complete a report, even though not all students have access to computers at home. Students without home access must use computers in the department offices or in the FAMS lab to complete their assignments.

Although Renaissance students are particularly motivated to complete assignments given in core subject areas, they are ironically sometimes less driven in classes that actually involve computer use. For example, Gail Jones must constantly remind students in her journalism class to stay focused on their work for her class. Students often try to complete their homework for other classes, like chemistry or precalculus during journalism. Jones complains that students often take too many difficult classes, leaving them little time to focus in her class on learning about journalism, much less using the computers she has in her classroom. As a result, many of the computers in her class go unused on any given day, even though hers is one of the few classrooms with technology available for student use.

Student Interest in High-Tech Careers

Despite the lack of technology in the school, a number of Renaissance students are interested in or planning to pursue careers in technology. One girl writing for her Computer Applications class wrote that she wanted to be a Web designer, "probably because I live on the computer at home." She uses AOL and GirlPages to create her own Web pages at home, even though she receives no support or instruction in design at school. One scheduled class at Renaissance in Web design is run as a study hall, since access to the Internet within the school is so limited. Another senior we spoke to had just been admitted to the University of Michigan, where he plans to major in computer science. At Renaissance, he served as an aide to Lampi and took a full course load that included three AP classes. He rarely used technology at school, however, even though he had a computer at home and had begun to dabble in programming. When asked how he thought his technology skills would compare with those of other entering computer science students at the University of Michigan, he admitted, "I'll probably be behind them."

Administrators and teachers echo these concerns. Dr. Hamilton acknowledges that such students are falling behind "in terms of internships and working with business communities." Really technologically advanced students must "[take] advantage of the advanced computer class at Randolph [a nearby vocational-technical school run by the district]." Similarly, science teacher Turner argues, "Our students are not competitive because they do not have the things that are needed to be competitive, to learn, to gain from access to technologies and everybody else is ahead of them. It has nothing to do with their intelligence. They have the intelligence and they can do it."

In Spite of Excellence: A School Community with Many Needs

In addition to the external funding challenges that Renaissance has faced in acquiring new technologies to support student learning, several challenges at the school level for a long time hindered the school's efforts to provide technology access to students and to integrate technology more fully throughout the curriculum.

A Technology Coordinator with Many Hats

Unlike Murray-Wright, Renaissance High School did not have a single teacher assigned either to the main computer lab or to function as an official technology coordinator for the school at the time of our study. The FAMS lab was shared by three different teachers, none of whom has primary responsibility for the maintenance of the lab. Lilly Gladney's lab was used primarily to offer a district-required introductory computer course and a FAMS course and was not available for teaching other subjects. Phil Lampi, who took on the role of coordinating with business partners to acquire new technologies and pull together the technology plan for the school, had many other responsibilities in the school before he retired at the end of the 1999–2000 school year.

In addition to functioning as the school's de facto technology coordinator, Lampi was head of the Math Department. He taught a calculus class and also tutored and advised struggling students in math throughout the day. On multiple occasions during our visits, Lampi was called out to meet with parents, deal with student behavioral issues, and cover for teachers who were absent for the day. Rarely did Lampi have a day or even a regular part of each day to focus on technology. He wore many hats, of which being the primary person responsible for acquiring new technologies was only one.

A Principal with a Focus on Expansion

During the two years of our study, Renaissance's principal focused her efforts on an opportunity to acquire more space for the badly crowded school. The current building is small, and space is a constant problem when the school schedule is produced anew each semester. An adjacent hospital and training center are both considering selling their properties. Dr. Hamilton would like the district to purchase their buildings for Renaissance. She even had the FAMS students in Gladney's class work on this initiative by producing architectural designs.

The students designed blueprints for building a walkway between Renaissance and the adjacent buildings. The 3-D design was produced using the home computer of one of the students in the class. Students have now built two different scale models of the grounds and walkway using Legos to depict their own design as well as an alternative design preferred by Hamilton, which incorporates a new sports stadium. Hamilton was hopeful that the new buildings would allow Renaissance to develop new curriculum offerings, as well as permit more students in the current programs.

Curriculum Plans

Among the new curricular offerings that Hamilton hopes the school expansion will allow are a number of classes that will involve more technology. Hamilton plans to add a premedical college preparatory track that will include classes in medical techniques and biotechnology. She would also like to see new classes in PASCAL and

VisualBasic programming and in Computer-Assisted Design (CAD). The new offerings are all designed to provide a rigorous college preparatory program for students interested in preparing for careers in medicine or engineering.

Hamilton plans to make these curricular changes, even if the school is not successful in acquiring the adjacent hospital and training center. She has sought approval from the district to hire six new teachers for the new curriculum. If the school's capacity is not increased, this would require the district to amend its formula for funding teachers at a ratio of thirty-five students per teacher just for Renaissance. To teach the additional classes, the FAMS lab would have to be partitioned, and new equipment would have to be purchased. The new premedical and preengineering programs, if implemented, may help to make technology more a part of the core curriculum for many of Renaissance's highest-achieving students. At present, computer technology is used the most in electives that students take, mostly as "therapy" as one teacher put it, or as alternative homework and extra credit. For example, Gary Hudkins assigns computer-based homework in his economics class as an alternative to answering questions in the textbook. He makes the problems in the book harder to encourage students to do the computer-based homework. Similarly, Joe Bell uses technology assignments as extra credit in his classes, assigning students the task of finding out about some scientific phenomenon, such as identifying the oldest living thing on Earth or the largest land animal, on the Internet.

Although the proposed new curricula include courses that would teach students how to use specific software, they would not necessarily increase the frequency with which students learn *with* technology in academic courses on other topics.

Coda: A Corner Turned, Still Seeking More Technology

Phil Lampi's retirement at the end of the 1999–2000 school year created the need to identify someone else who could carry responsibility for implementing the technology plan at the school. The school decided to dedicate a staff person to the job of technology teacher and fill a new district-created position with a certified teacher. The decision has already proven to be a wise one, as the school has begun to turn a corner in acquiring new technologies to match its talented and eager students.

Renaissance benefited from the creation of a district-funded position for each school focused on technology. Renaissance at last got a single staff person who could dedicate his time to technology. Over the summer of 2000, Renaissance found Bob Fadden, a teacher with eight years at Cooley High School and experience with multimedia from industry, to take on this role. At Cooley, Fadden's job involved teaming students with teachers who had specific technology needs. For example, a classroom teacher might need a PowerPoint presentation for a lecture, and Fadden would work with students and the classroom teacher to produce the presentation. His metrics at Cooley for these multimedia projects were simple and driven by the kinds of assessments used in business. He requires students to be able to answer yes to the following three questions: "Does it do what I ask?" "Did you do it on time?" and "Does it work?"

Fadden is helped in his mission by ten new iBooks provided by the district that have been networked to a new wireless LAN. These iBooks are loaded with advanced multimedia software and can go with students into class as they work on specific projects. Back in the FAMS lab, students can do even more with the equipment Fadden has helped the school acquire—a video production system, new color printer, and a digital camera. In his first year at Renaissance, Fadden began working with classroom teachers like Joe Bell to involve students in learning HyperStudio and PowerPoint to produce presentations of their work, and he has plans for creating teacher-student teams at Renaissance similar to those he developed at Cooley. There is still a need to add computers to the school's many classrooms, Fadden points out, but Fadden has a commitment to expanding the curriculum offerings in technology in the meantime and continuing the struggle to help Renaissance find more and more powerful equipment for the school.

Although the school continues to try to acquire new technologies and connect more classrooms to the Internet, Renaissance High School remains subject to the many institutional forces that have kept the school from providing the level of technology access available at other schools in the district. Funding formulas and budget limitations leave Renaissance with little discretionary funding that can be used for buying computers. At the same time, Renaissance has an important new resource in Bob Fadden that can help to overcome these obstacles. As our observations at the other schools in this study have shown, the presence of a technology champion at an urban school, in the form of a principal or teacher-leader dedicated to technology or a strong technology coordinator, is critical in helping gain technology access for students and in helping to set a vision for technology use in the school. The road ahead for Fadden will surely be challenging, but his own experience and commitment to seeing students learn with technology will certainly go far as Renaissance strives to provide a technology infrastructure worthy of its students.

7

Show Them How
We're Learning

STUDENTS AT THE TECH CENTER

"I've noticed that it made me feel good about teaching. I learned something that other people didn't know about, teaching other people how to learn to program. It's exciting. I learned how to use digital cameras and so much about new technology. It's fun." These words express a sentiment shared by many a teacher who has discovered the power of technology to transform classroom instruction. The recognition that bringing technology into the classroom can support one's own discovery and learning process as well as that of one's students has motivated many teachers' pursuit of technology skills.

But these are actually the words of a student at Mumford High School in Detroit, who has been working all day with a group of seniors in her community to teach them how to use technology. About half of her elderly students have never used computers before, and many more have only limited experience. This student's job for the day included taking pictures of each of the students in the class with her digital camera, giving them a diskette with their picture, and helping them to open their pictures in an application program.

She has learned much this day about her students and about her own skills and abilities as a technology user: "It surprises me, the fact that it's like they aren't thirteen because they are adults and for a child to learn before you know something that adults don't. It's kinda surprising and it feels good because . . . that you learned something that someone else didn't know and it feels good to teach them and pass it on down. Show them how we're learning and how I learned."

This student's experience is hardly unique at Mumford. Each day a cadre of students help their peers in the school's Technology Center (called the "Tech Center" by everyone at Mumford) learn how to use technology. And the Tech Center itself is a hub within this vibrant school community, a nexus of activity where teachers, students, parents, and community all come together to learn alongside one another.

A Technology Center at the Hub of a Connected School Community

Mumford High School is close to the north-central border of Detroit. The neighborhood surrounding Mumford is an African American working- and lower-middle-class neighborhood, consisting of small single-family homes along the side streets. The main thoroughfare within the neighborhood, Wyoming Avenue, has a number of boarded up storefronts and struggling small businesses. But despite the run-down appearance of the local commercial area, Mumford is described by one of the assistant principals not as an "inner inner-city" school, but rather as an urban school in a neighborhood with families connected to the school and strong local organizations and institutions.

The school serves some sixteen hundred students in grades 9 through 12 and is described by the principal as a "comprehensive" high school. According to one student, "when parents or older people look at this school they think it's good because we have computers and we're the number one Compact school," referring to the Detroit Compact program, a college preparatory partnership with area businesses designed to increase the number of college-bound students in Detroit through scholarships. It is the Compact program that was responsible for bringing the Tech Center to Mumford and making technology a key part of the school's identity. According to students and teachers across the district, Mumford and "technology" are synonymous.

The Detroit Compact is a partnership between Detroit businesses, institutions of higher education, and the city schools, established to design and implement strategies to increase student test scores and make sure they would be prepared both for higher education and the world of work. When Mumford became a part of the Compact in 1989, the program joined with Ameritech and Detroit Public Schools (DPS) to build a technology center within the school. Funding for the center came from the Ameritech Foundation, Michigan Bell (now Ameritech), the Compact, and the DPS. Michigan Bell coordinated construction of the room, and ongoing support was provided by Ameritech, Wayne State University, and Wayne County Regional Educational Services Administration (RESA).

Valeria Hatten, the school's union representative, served on Mumford's original technology steering committee that began planning the way in which technology would be implemented at Mumford. She said that several committee members, including her, were selected to visit a variety of sites throughout southeastern Michigan as part of designing the Technology Center. The goal was to have them visit schools during a six-month period, then report to others about what they thought was needed. She recalled, "We were able to come back and provide our own personal experience of what we saw, what we learned, what we thought would be useful here at Mumford and from there they were able to put together [the plan]."

Since the beginning the Tech Center has allowed students to develop technology skills through projects in all subject areas. It has developed a strong reputation within the district because of the visibility of the Compact program, the inclusive planning process, and the center's director, Claudia Burton, who serves as the school's technology coordinator. According to the principal, Linda Spight, the school is known for its technology because of the way it was approached: "In terms of having a person, and having a committee, and trying to infuse it. . . . Our reputation is such that we are the technology school in the district. We don't have as much technology as we would want, but we try to maximize the use of the technology that we have."

In fact, the school has been creative and successful in using what technology it has, and the Tech Center has been the hub of activity for a close-knit school community that puts students at the center. The Tech Center at Mumford is a good illustration of how technology can serve as a focal point for providing students with opportunities to participate in building and maintaining relationships within the school and contributing to the greater community.

A Place Open to the Community

During the school week, Mumford's Tech Center is open all day long. Each academic department is allotted a certain number of weeks per semester to use the lab, and individual teachers within departments sign up with their department heads for particular time slots for projects, often several weeks in advance. The center is also open three afternoons a week until 6 P.M. for teachers and students. Many students take advantage of the after-school hours to check e-mail, surf the Web, or finish projects they began in class.

In any given week, a number of teachers from other schools, visiting students, parents, and community members may also pass through the Tech Center. For example, teachers from across the city may come for an afternoon professional development session on how to use the Internet. The student Technology Club may hold its weekly meeting to plan for an upcoming fundraiser. Or a community group may use the center as a training site for its members. One of Principal Spight's goals for the Tech Center is that it be utilized as much as possible and that it be a part of the wider neighborhood and community.

The Family Tree Maker Project

A particularly strong example of how the Technology Center serves as a hub for activity within the school and its surrounding community is the Family Tree Project, initiated in the summer of 1999. That summer the president of the Fred Hart Williams Genealogical Society, Peggy Sawyer-Williams, approached Claudia Burton, the technology coordinator at Mumford, about using the Tech Center to teach society members how to use a new genealogy software program, Family Tree Maker. The society has some two hundred to three hundred members and is the second largest African American genealogical society in the United States.

Burton suggested that she and the Mumford Technology Club members could together host a series of workshops in parallel with the society's own monthly meetings for those members interested in learning more about computers. Many of the genealogical society members had close ties to Mumford. One of the members had a son who had recently graduated from Mumford and was completing a computer science degree from Oakland University. Others had extended family members with connections to Mumford or lived close by the school.

After school started, to prepare for the society's first meeting at the Tech Center, Burton spent three weeks teaching the basics of the Family Tree Maker program to the members of her student Technology Club. The club includes a number of ninth graders with limited technology experience, so the preparation time they spent together was critical, according to Burton. Also important was the time she had spent conducting what she calls "computer literacy" training with the students; they learned how to use the Windows operating system and how to take good care of the hardware in the Tech Center.

When the Fred Hart Williams Genealogical Society members arrived for the first of several Saturday meetings in the Tech Center on a Saturday morning in October, they were warmly greeted outside the building by Technology Club members and officers. The day began with refreshments for society members in an "anteroom" of the Tech Center, a room with desks for students and pictures of the Tech Center when it first opened. The Tech Center itself and the anteroom differ significantly in form, function, and feel. The anteroom has no computers; it serves as a place where instructions are given and where students can transition to the business-like attitude and demeanor that are required in the lab itself. Food and drink can be enjoyed in the anteroom, but not in the Tech Center. These norms were applied to the genealogical society members, just as they were to students.

Burton asked the Mumford students, who stood in front of the anteroom, to introduce themselves and indicate their grade levels. Next she outlined the schedule for the day and instructed each society member to find a computer. After a few minutes, when everyone had identified a computer and a youth assistant had been assigned to groups of four society members, Burton asked for a show of hands of society members who felt they knew everything they needed to know about computers to use the software. No hands went up. She then asked for a show of hands of people who knew anything about computers, and only six hands went up.

Burton instructed the society members to open the Family Tree Maker program and worked with them on how to use the mouse. She showed them how to open the program by moving the cursor to the start bar, clicking, and releasing the mouse on the desired program. The student assistants helped the genealogical society members get settled on their computers and troubleshot problems with opening the program. Next Burton dimmed the lights and used a large overhead projection screen to show the society members the main page for the program. She provided data for them to enter about Abraham Lincoln, and as she showed the different elements, the adults began to practice on their own.

The adults needed a great deal of help from their young mentors. They had trouble aligning the cursor with the fields and were particularly prone to getting error messages back from incorrect entries. They had problems entering dates, using the Caps Lock function instead of shifting, and with using tabs. The tech assistants patiently supported them and gained confidence in their own skill level through helping the adults. When one of the adults finished early, his technical assistant showed him how to start Netscape and access the main Mumford page. In interviews with researchers, the students expressed some surprise at the adults' rudimentary skill level. "They didn't know the Internet," remarked one girl. "Everybody knows the Internet."

After forty-five minutes of practice, Burton excused the adults for a break. Most continued to work for five to ten minutes, eating into their fifteen-minute scheduled break. The adults and youth were working away at entering the data provided and did not seem to mind that their break had been shortened.

In the second half of the session, Burton dimmed the lights again and reviewed with the group how to cut and paste sections of text within the software Notes that could be created for each family member entered into the database. Next she showed how to import pictures. Each society member was given a diskette with an image of Abraham Lincoln on it saved as a picture file. The diskette also had a digital photo of the society member, taken by one of the tech assistants. They used these diskettes to import pictures of themselves into the Family Tree Maker program.

At the end of the session, Burton closed the society meeting and thanked everyone for coming. The young assistants immediately began to turn off computers and cover each computer with a plastic sheet. After the society members thanked the young people for their help, Burton held an impromptu debriefing for the students. The students felt the day had gone well, and Burton concurred, "Pat yourself on the back, everybody." She also talked with the group about strategies for handling the problems that inevitably arise when using technology. "If something is going wrong with one computer, and it's clear that it's beyond what you can take care of, don't just come to me. I may be teaching or whatever, so it's important to do something like encourage two people to share a computer for a while, if necessary." She told the students that their next step would be to learn People Find, the CD-ROM database. She adds, "Keep looking for a movie, guys," referring to the annual event that raises funds for the Tech Center. To close, Burton asked a group of youth to do a "light check" and equipment check. They went back to the lab and turned out lights and checked the AV command console in the back office. Through such actions, Burton reinforces her Technology Club members' sense of responsibility for maintaining and caring for the Tech Center.

Connecting Back to the Curriculum

In the close-knit community of Mumford High, projects often have "legs" — extensions to other school activities and practices. When they heard about the Family Tree Maker project Burton was coordinating, two other Mumford teachers saw connections between their own curricular goals and constructing family trees. Burton collaborated with the two teachers to arrange for their students to learn how to use the program during their allotted time in the Tech Center.

One teacher had her English class use the Family Tree Maker program in conjunction with conducting Internet research on the writers of the Harlem Renaissance. Students in her class were asked to trace their own ancestry back to grandparents and great-grandparents who were alive during that time. This teacher was hopeful that her students would later appreciate the work they had done to research their own family's history. Since tools like the Family Tree Maker were not available when she was a student, she could not imagine having the opportunity to scan in pictures and create electronic records of conversations with her own family's "historian."

A social studies teacher taught a course on African American History for the first time beginning in fall of 1999. The class is an elective, composed mostly of seniors. In the first semester of the class, students studied African kingdoms of the seventeenth and eighteenth centuries, the slave trade, the European colonial powers, and slavery in the United States. In planning for the course, the teacher decided to use the movie *Roots* as a unifying theme. Students used a district-provided textbook four days a week, and on Fridays, they watched a segment of *Roots* to ground the facts they had learned in the different stories of the Alex Haley series.

When the teacher learned that Burton had a program that would allow students to trace their own family's ancestry, he jumped on the opportunity to have them learn the program as part of their class project. He wanted his students to connect what they were learning about African American history to their own families' experience: "It's important to know who you are, to have a sense of pride, self-esteem, to have knowledge and learning about what's important. Everybody's family is part of history-making, and I want my students to know that. . . . You had a place. Your family has contributed to what America is."

Central Role of Students in the Tech Center

Evident in the use of Family Tree Maker with the genealogical society and in projects for regular classes are two educational reform features that researchers have found characterize schools that have successfully integrated technology into the curriculum. First, students have the opportunity to play the role of teacher to other students and to adults, deepening their own learning as they help others. Second, students have the opportunity to make connections between what they are learning in school and their own experience and identities. Students draw on their own families' "funds of knowledge" (Moll, Amanti, Neff, & Gonzalez, 1992) to complete their assignments and relate the material they are learning in class to their own lives.

Yet another way that the Tech Center supports learning is through the many opportunities students have for *informal* learning through their participation in activities of the Tech Center. Learning, in other words, is not always planned but is occurring all the time in different corners of the room. As one teacher said,

Learning is happening all the time. In the classroom it's more of a two-tier kind of a situation where I'm imparting knowledge to you and you are taking in that knowledge and you're giving me feedback. Whereas in the lab, everybody's learning and learning is occurring constantly, all the time. . . . "I found this" . . . "look at this" . . . "let me explore this new idea even further" . . . "what do you think if I did this" . . . so it's more independent, critical thinking on the student's part, more so than what you see in the classroom.

At any one time during the day, there may be two classes and groups of students working on different projects in the lab at the same time. Although particular classes are scheduled during each hour, there are always a number of drop-ins when space is available. The room is neither quiet nor loud—sometimes Burton plays light jazz through the sound system in the room. Mixed into this informality, however, is an overarching atmosphere that Burton and Hicks, an alternative education teacher, describe as "a professional environment." Burton said that it is important that you have a "calm personality" to run a technology center like Mumford's: "You're dealing with a lot of kids and four or five different things are going on at the same time."

Maintaining an Office Attitude

Just as at Murray-Wright, the physical condition of the computer labs is better than that of many of the regular classrooms. At Mumford, the Tech Center gleams. The room is one of the few rooms in the school that is carpeted, and the paint is much fresher than can be found in other rooms or on the outside of the school. The room is a large space and contains forty-three IBM Windows machines, many of which were purchased in 1999 through a grant from Ameritech Foundation and through Principal Spight's budgeting prowess. Seven Macintoshes sit in the back corner of the room. All the computers are networked, and the school has a T-1 line that connects them to the Internet.

When they come into the Center, students must leave all their bags, sodas, and food in the anteroom that sits adjacent to the lab. In a typical class session, students first spend time in the anteroom getting settled down, hearing instructions from Burton or their classroom teacher. When they enter the Tech Center proper, students are required to act as if they were in a place of work. One student said, "When we come to the Tech Center, Ms. Burton makes us keep an office attitude—we can't chew gum, or fool around in our chair, or talk, or put our feet on stuff." Perhaps surprisingly, students appear to recognize the value of this approach: "You can use that attitude when you get older."

For the most part, students are remarkably conscientious about maintaining this office demeanor in the Tech Center. The care and concern for the computers and the room that the students show no doubt contribute to the fact that nearly all of the computers are up and running all the time in the Tech Center. A group of students Burton has trained to act as her assistants also plays a central role in caretaking the computers.

Applications Specialists in the Lab

Burton depends on students to help her maintain the cleanliness of the Tech Center and assist other students when they encounter what one teacher referred to as "minor glitches." The students who work as Burton's assistants are either members of the school's Technology Club or students who work in the Tech Center as "application specialists." The students who work with Burton not only gain technology skills, according to Principal Spight, but also get the experience of "being troubleshooters and helping others."

Burton's applications specialists must all go through extensive training in basic care of computers and in using many of the programs that classes use regularly. Burton trains these specialists to "walk the room," checking to see if anyone needs help and making sure that students are on task and that computers are all in working order. She also trains them in using different search engines to help other students conduct research on the Internet and talks to them about what different search engines can do. Teachers say they can rely on these students for solving small, routine problems their students encounter and to provide them with assistance as they work on their individual projects.

Researchers observed one applications specialist helping a student in an English class find out who was president during the 1940s. Many of these students had not used the Internet extensively and were having trouble finding the right search engine. Two of Burton's applications specialists for the hour leapt into action, helping several students open Netscape and type in the URL for Infoseek and Webcrawler. They helped the students in the class identify search terms they could use to find out who was president, taking care to look at students nearby, to see if they had discovered a URL that might help locate the desired information. The student applications specialists explained how to look at the hits that were returned by the search engine and to think about which ones might have the answer.

The applications specialists were critical to the English students' success in finding the answer to the question the classroom teacher had posed. They were able to be many places at once, where the teacher might have been able to help only one student at a time. The applications specialists provided strategic assistance to students, modeling the use of search strategies and showing students how to think through how to use the search hits to answer a research question. Although in this case, the research question was a factual one that the students in the English class might have answered using a history textbook, the activity illustrates the important role the student applications specialists play in supporting regular classroom teachers' use of the Tech Center.

The Technology Club

The students who worked with the Fred Hart Williams Genealogical Society were all members of the student-governed Technology Club facilitated by Claudia Burton. This after-school club provides Mumford students with opportunities to develop problem-solving and decision-making skills through planning activities such as fundraisers or field trips to local companies or museums. The club is the student voice for the Center, and student participants often are among the lab's application specialists who work in the Center during the day. Students in the Center participate and help coordinate (with Burton's leadership) fundraisers for the club, field trips, and a video they are producing on technology use in the workplace.

Burton takes a strong facilitative role within the club's regular meetings. Students have opportunities to make decisions along the way, and in one meeting attended by SRI researchers, Burton shared information about the amount of money the Club raised for the Tech Center from their various fundraisers. Although Burton provides the club's overall direction, students have a key role in making decisions about how to spend a portion of the money raised and about the kinds of activities they will do together.

Just as in many kinds of after-school programs that are typically housed in community-based organizations (e.g., Heath & McLaughlin, 1993), in the Technology Club, students can develop different kinds of relationships with adults than are normally found in classrooms. In the club Burton places herself in a different relation to the students—as someone who, like them, is interested in generating strategies and ideas for supporting technology in the school. Students, not the teacher, ultimately got to decide what the fundraiser would be and what they would do with the money they earned. Club members were guided, but not directed, by Burton's own sense of possibilities and constraints.

Developing Students' Motivation and Identity

Putting students at the center of technology-supported curricular activities gives students a reason to be more engaged with learning at Mumford and to develop a sense of themselves as competent, contributing members of the school community. According to one student, "When the teacher is talking, you get bored and fall asleep. With the computer you're doing what you want to do and focusing on what you want to hear."

Lauren Randall, a special education teacher, noted that when she has signed up for her class to use the Tech Center, more students come to class: "In high school you have poor attendance but I notice in the Tech Center more students come to class. They love it. . . . They love being here and using the computers."

Teacher Valeria Hatten cited increased ownership over the learning process brought about by the ability to access information through the Internet as one important source of increased motivation to learn. Students, too, cited increased motivation as a benefit of technology use. "It's a different way of doing things," said one. "It's a lot easier than always being in class," said another, citing technology as a tool for increasing student motivation for learning.

Laconda Hicks believes that the atmosphere of the Tech Center contributes to a sense of importance and professionalism within the school. Students feel they are doing engaging work when they are in the Tech Center and thus feel better about themselves. The special education teachers noted that technology was especially helpful in working with their students because they are more comfortable in working with computers. Randall notes that "a book is intimidating to a lot of our students." They witnessed students' increased self-esteem through being able to generate products they would not have been able to produce before.

Projects such as building family trees, as implemented in the African American history class, do more than just motivate students and inspire better student work. For the teacher and his students, the projects became explorations in cultural identity. The teacher's goal for his students included an expanded knowledge of African American history and the development of an identity as a person of worth, whose families and ancestors have contributed to the building of America. Tying the students' learning and projects to significant moments in African American history, and linking those moments back to students' own families encourage students to see the continuities among the personal, cultural, and historical aspects of what it means to be a young African American growing up in Detroit at the beginning of the twenty-first century.

Leadership from a Dynamic Technology Coordinator

That many of the projects that teachers lead with their students are aimed at engaging students with their own learning is no surprise, given the origins of Technology Coordinator Claudia Burton's own introduction to the power of using technology in schools. Some years ago, as an elementary school librarian, Burton was trying to help a boy whom other teachers referred to as a "Do-drop-in" student because of his erratic attendance and propensity to sleep in class. Burton told him to try to compose a letter on her computer. He did so and printed it. Burton's epiphany occurred when she saw the pride on his face as he gave her the completed letter. She cites this experience as the moment when she saw the potential of technology to transform students' self-esteem and motivation in school.

Her belief in the power of technology thus sparked, Burton jumped at the opportunity when she was asked in 1991 to be head of the new Tech Center at Mumford. Prior to coming to Mumford, she had made a name for herself as the librarian who created the first electronic catalog for a high school library in Detroit. When she arrived at her new school, she was provided with a budget to maintain the lab, including funds that were saved when the school decided not to purchase a costly integrated learning system. Since that time Burton has coordinated with independent technology support providers to keep the lab up and running. Burton says her role is "to make sure that the software's working, the hardware's working, and that there's an environment conducive to learning." She works with a technology steering committee composed of teachers from every department who make decisions about the lab and are involved in the scheduling of classes' access to the lab.

Perhaps no one has been a more tireless advocate for technology at Mumford than Burton, who has been active ever since coming to Mumford in ensuring that the initial business partners who built the lab maintained their commitment to supporting it. Because of her efforts the Ameritech Foundation, one of the key early players in the effort, recognized Burton with the Ameritech Technology Teacher Excellence Award in 1997 for her efforts in running the Tech Center at the school. Ameritech (the company) has also continued to provide technical support to the school on an as-needed basis. "They're right there," she says, "if something goes wrong."

In addition to cultivating these business partnerships, Burton has been involved in raising funds within the school to ensure that the Tech Center has everything it needs to keep functioning, including peripherals and expendable items like printer cartridges, which are expensive and difficult to pay for out of the school's main budget. She has even involved her students in the Tech Center in writing grants to bring more technology to the school.

Burton's role in making the Tech Center so successful cannot be underestimated. She spends after-school hours and many weekends at the Tech Center, donating time and energy for which she is not paid. She trains teachers, students, and community members. She assists teachers with classroom instruction, teaching particular applications and Internet search skills to students when teachers themselves do not necessarily have the skills. She manages the hardware, servers, and network connections throughout the school, not just in the Tech Center. She cobbles together funds to help pay for ongoing technical support and to keep her technology current and develops new connections and partnerships with business and the community to keep the learning fresh and exciting.

When we talked to Burton about the DPS concern that technology-savvy teachers such as herself are being lured to the suburbs where salaries are higher and technology resources and upkeep easier to come by, she demurred. While acknowledging the attractiveness of suburban pastures for others, Burton insists, "I'm on a mission here." Without Claudia Burton—or a comparable leader performing the myriad of tasks she does—Mumford's Tech Center would be an empty room full of aging computers rather than a thriving center of learning within the school.

A Strong Professional Community of Teachers

Although Burton is an essential element in technology use at Mumford, her work does not occur in a vacuum. She is supported by an active principal and a strong professional community of teachers committed to the students of the school. The climate of collegiality and high expectations observed in the Center permeates the school as a whole. Principal Spight believes this climate of collegiality is part of what brought the Tech Center to Mumford in the first place.

Each of the teachers we interviewed who had been at Mumford for more than five years described the previous principals and Spight as fostering an atmosphere of collegiality and collaboration among teachers. The friendliness, mutual respect, and supportive environment were evident throughout the school. The current principal believes her role is to continue to foster this spirit of collaboration. In addition, teachers are self-directed in their motivation for continuous improvement, particularly in regard to technology. In this quintessential union town, Mumford teachers are willing to put in extra time to learn new tools that strengthen their ability to teach with technology.

When asked "Why technology?" most Mumford teachers interviewed looked at the researchers with surprise. To them, technology should be a required component of learning for all students, integrated throughout the curriculum. They believe that we all live in a technological society and that students need to be prepared for the world they live in. Their role is to put the effort into learning that technology so that their students can as well.

One incentive for Mumford teachers to learn the technology themselves has been Burton's rule that teachers must take technology training themselves before they can schedule their class into the Tech Center. (She has relaxed the rule with new teachers who come with training in technology from preservice education.) Ongoing after-school training sessions are led by Burton, other teachers, and outside consultants on different applications (word processing, spreadsheets, presentation), use of the Internet for research, e-mail, and Web page design. Burton limits each session to thirty, to ensure enough individualized instruction. Laconda Hicks mentioned that lately these workshops have been in high demand. "She puts the notice in your box and if you don't return it quickly you don't get in," Hicks said. "They're unpaid, they're after school, and people come just to find out how to do this—just to learn." Teachers at Mumford are also involved in training their colleagues districtwide. About twenty district technology professional development sessions were held last year in the Tech Center because of its superior training facilities, which include a ten-foot by ten-foot projection screen and wireless sound system.

Perhaps the most common use of the Tech Center among teachers is for short-term student research projects that require Internet research. Hicks, a special education teacher in math and computer sciences, gave her students the assignment of planning a trip. She provided students with a budget and students conducted research on the Internet to determine the cost of flights, meals, and hotels and to find things to do while on their trip. Last year a teacher had his Government students in the lab three days per term (plus additional time for individual students when space is available in the Center), researching information on the Internet regarding famous court cases. These and other teachers typically have their students come in for one or two sessions at the Tech Center to search the Internet and then have students analyze their research to complete reports and research papers for class.

Challenges to Integrating Technology Across the Curriculum

Despite Mumford's successes, the school has faced several challenges as it has tried to integrate technology into classrooms outside the Tech Center. Problems with older equipment in regular classrooms, limited access to the Tech Center, and a lack of adequate technical support are all factors that have constrained the uses classroom teachers have made of technology.

Aging Equipment

Beyond the walls of the Tech Center, only a few investments have been made in new hardware for classrooms. Those classrooms that do have computers have computers with inadequate memory to run current operating systems and productivity software such as word processors, spreadsheets, and databases. As of spring of 2000, in the classroom where the district-required Computer Applications class is taught, there is a network of 486 computers donated by EDS that run Windows 95. Before the current school year, the library had five working computers (three were broken) used primarily for word processing. In 1999 Principal Spight found funds to replace these computers with ten new computers installed by Learning Consultants (the same business partner that built the labs at Murray-Wright). Another ten computers were purchased in fall of 2000. Although these computers are connected to the Internet, the high traffic on the district Web server makes connections slow; the Web server downtown, intended to support five hundred computers, is being used to support close to five thousand. The yearbook staff works in a small room off the library, where Burton has put ten G3 Macintoshes that used to be in the Tech Center.

By and large, most Mumford classrooms have no computers at all and those that do have computers have one to five older pieces of equipment. One of the obstacles to purchasing new computers for classroom use is cost, and the cost of purchasing new computers is only part of the problem. Claudia Burton noted that since theft is a risk, any time new equipment is purchased, a special secure door, costing upwards of $900, must be installed for the classroom. If the classroom is on the first floor, moreover, bars must be put on the windows so passersby cannot break the windows and steal the computers. Burton says that this year the school may be able to relax this requirement, since the district has decided to put surveillance cameras in all Detroit schools.

Limited Access to the Tech Center
Limits Extended Student Projects

Since the Tech Center is the only place where an entire class of students can work one to a computer in the school, and since each teacher may get only one week of time per semester in the Tech Center with his or her class, students can rarely engage in extended computer-supported projects or inquiry. Although students can access the Tech Center after school throughout a project, it is far more typical for classes to work in the Tech Center when they are at the beginning or end of a project, when they are researching or producing a final written project.

A class project in Algebra II is typical. Students were required to develop a working hypothesis on a scientific question of interest to them. Topics students chose ranged from testing the durability of different countertop materials to surveying students about which of two Disney characters they liked more. The projects took about two to three weeks to complete. Students spent only one class period in the Tech Center near the end of the project using MS Excel to generate graphs and MS Word to design the text of their presentations. The text and graphs were then cut into sections for their foam board triptychs.

The students whom researchers interviewed gave the following examples of technology-related work, all of which suggest short-term projects rather than extended inquiry:

- Biology—creating PowerPoint slides for a presentation
- Geography—learning about different parts of the world on the Internet
- Entrepreneurship—looking at different types of businesses on the Internet

When asked where they learned how to use technology, most students with whom researchers spoke said that they did not learn how to use technology here at Mumford, but at home, where they have more access to technology. With more points of access in school, one wonders whether those students without home access—and perhaps some who do have computers at home—might have answered this question differently.

Lack of Adequate Technical Support

When the Tech Center was first installed, Ameritech provided a great deal of technical support on demand. Support technicians were available within the day to solve any problems that arose. Since the formal partnership with the Ameritech Foundation ended, securing adequate technical support has been a struggle. According to Spight, the school continues to pay for outside technical support through school funds and the proceeds of fundraisers. However, this support is only for the equipment in the Tech Center. Spight added that the computers that are not in the lab are more of a problem "because when they're down we don't always get the technical support we need when we need it. It comes, but it doesn't come quickly enough, and when you're talking about student achievement, you need them to be ready all of the time." The school depends on district support for any major problems. Administrative uses of technology get higher priority than educational uses within the district's system. Money and personnel are the bottom line, notes Burton, and the district's technical support is underfunded. She reported in November 1999 having waited since the winter holiday break in 1998 to get a new file server up and running.

In addition, DPS has a policy of not maintaining older machines such as those found throughout Mumford. Mumford's own staff must make repairs for the many older machines in the building. According to Burton, "It's a nightmare when you have old equipment. . . . It's a nightmare as to what we're going to do to keep the equipment up and running and functioning as the new stuff comes in. [We have to ask] 'Can you configure the new stuff to run the old stuff?' and 'Is it cost effective to get someone in here?'"

That leaves Burton to fix most of the small problems herself—especially on the older machines—and most teachers believe she cannot possibly do it all herself. One teacher suggested the need for more technical support on-site.

A's Communications, a district contractor, does help with installing programs and with basic maintenance of computers throughout the building, but they are not available all day long. One of the assistant principals has just lined up a recent high school graduate to fill in some of the gaps in technical support.

Limited Discretionary Funds for Buying Technology

All the teachers interviewed by researchers want more funds available to provide computers for their classrooms. Spight noted the challenge of acquiring funds for the expenses that are associated with computers. She said many of the grants that are available would not allow the funds to go toward the technology infrastructure, such as wiring and security. "Some people don't understand that when you're talking about technology, you're not just talking about the computers, you're talking about everything else that goes along with it," she said. "That's what has been frustrating—not really having a budget sufficient enough to do what I think needs to be done."

One of the problems the school faces is that its discretionary funds from federal Title I and Michigan 31A compensatory education programs are more limited than at a school like Murray-Wright. As technology is not a line item from the district that is awarded to each school, schools must typically rely on federal and state dollars awarded to schools on the basis of the percentage of students who are eligible for free or reduced-price lunches. That means high-poverty schools get more discretionary funds that in many cases go toward buying technology, a strategy that Murray-Wright has used effectively. As less than a third of the students at Mumford are on record as coming from low-income families, the school receives a smaller share of federal and state dollars than most other high schools in the city. Small grants from foundations, bake sales, movies, and other fundraisers then must make up the difference, but these sources of funding cannot compare with the hundreds of thousands of dollars schools often receive through Title I and Michigan's 31A fund. One of the greatest challenges to writing grants, notes Burton, is that there are typically limitations on purchasing equipment through grants for which she applies. Schools need more flexibility, she notes, in how they spend money: "A lot of people who don't work in schools just don't realize that we can't keep track of new technology."

Plans for the Future

The school's overall goal remains the integration of technology throughout the curriculum, in alignment with the district's own plan for integrating technology standards across all subject areas. Ultimately, Principal Spight would like to have technology integrated "so that it becomes a natural fit and not something that's superimposed upon the existing curriculum." She added that teachers will soon be required to use technology as a management tool as the districtwide grading system begins to be implemented. This new system will require teachers to input their own grades directly into the computer.

Getting more computers into classrooms is also a focus of Mumford's technology plan. A technology steering committee composed of teachers from all departments helps set the direction of the school with regard to technology. The committee meets regularly, according to Burton, and recently has focused on getting more computers into classrooms for teachers to use. Valeria Hatten mentioned that she thinks that it is critical to have four or five computers in every classroom. Principal Spight agreed, saying, "Even though the Tech Center is a very valuable resource in the school, ultimately the computers need to be in the classroom if students are really going to get the maximum use out of them."

This year Mumford won a new grant from Ameritech Foundation that provided for funding technology curriculum integration. This allowed Burton to move a number of good computers upstairs into the Computer Applications lab, where most of the computers needed to be upgraded. She continues to plan fundraisers and seek grant opportunities that will help her acquire more technology to spread throughout the school.

In fall of 1999 the faculty and parents began a process to apply for permission from the district to move to a block schedule. Most teachers with whom researchers spoke saw this as a positive development, and thus far, according to Spight, the faculty is 90 percent in favor of the plan. These teachers view block scheduling as an opportunity to implement more extended project-based learning in their classrooms. Burton believes it will be especially beneficial for students using the Tech Center, because students will have much larger blocks of time to work on projects. A final vote took place in winter of 1999, and training will begin in May, using district professional development funds.

Mumford's Tech Center and its planning process are considered a model in Detroit, and our research has confirmed what many have noted previously. The Center has dynamic leadership and engages students in the joy of learning with technology. Despite the challenges of aging machines and limited technical support, Mumford stands as an example of what a school with limited funding but a committed team of teachers led by a technology coordinator can do, especially when they involve students in the process. Students really are at the center at the Tech Center, helping out and taking responsibility not just for their own learning but for maintaining the school's vision and leadership in using technology.

8

Summing Up

TECHNOLOGY USE IN
URBAN HIGH SCHOOLS

In presenting our portraits of technology use in six urban high schools, we have emphasized those uses of technology within the school that conform more closely to our concept of student-empowering technology use presented in Chapter One. These uses

- emulate the ways in which professionals use technology,
- involve complex tasks,
- require significant amounts of time for completion,
- give students latitude in designing their own products and in determining when and how to use technology,
- involve multiple academic disciplines, and
- provide opportunities for student collaboration with peers and outside experts.

Although by no means the norm, this kind of technology use can be found in urban high schools, as documented in our case studies. Applied mathematics teacher Stanley Henry's Winter Break Blues Project, for example, illustrates many of these features of student-empowering technology uses. Henry's ninth- and tenth-grade students were given a problem to solve—figure out the best week for the winter school break—but no explicit directions on how to solve it. Only through class discussion did the goal of saving on heating costs emerge as the criterion for choosing a specific week in February for the break. At this point, Henry's students realized that they needed data to determine when the coldest days could be expected to occur, and they turned to the Internet to find the data they needed to arrive at a recommendation. After pulling down fifty years of local temperature data, the students used spreadsheet software to store, organize, analyze, and graphically display the data. The data enabled them to draw a conclusion concerning the most logical break week, and the students then used PowerPoint to develop a presentation describing their project and their conclusions for presentation at the school's Family Night.

The Winter Break task was complex; it combined the disciplines of mathematics, science, and composition; it occurred over a significant amount of time and was largely shaped by student choices and decisions. Students worked with each other and with outside resources (e.g., local weather stations, the school's building engineer), and they figured out how to use the technology tools in ways that supported their research, decision making, and presentation.

It should be clear that such student-empowering uses of technology are not representative of technology use in urban high schools generally. Rather, such activities were pockets of student-centered technology use that stood out in schools that were already selected for their better-than-average readiness to use technology in interesting ways. Student-empowering uses of technology are not "business as usual" in these high schools. Glowing accounts of leading-edge uses of technology notwithstanding, the kinds of technology-supported practices we have emphasized are the exception rather than the rule in high schools generally. Although student-empowering uses of technology appear to be more common in schools serving high-achieving and more affluent students, they are hardly pervasive. Teacher reports on Becker's 1998 survey indicate that in the 1997–98 school year fewer than one out of five teachers had their students use the World Wide Web for ten or more lessons and fewer than one out of ten had students use simulations or exploratory environments, spreadsheets or databases, or multimedia or presentation software with that level of frequency (Becker, Ravitz, & Wong, 1999).

Barriers: Why Aren't Student-Empowering Uses of Technology More Common?

Much has been written in recent years on teachers' relatively low level of technology integration into their instruction. Generally cited causes for that low level of use (and areas where policymakers have sought to make changes) include

- lack of a technology infrastructure,
- lack of technical support,
- teacher discomfort with technology,
- scarcity of high-quality digital content in many subject areas,
- lack of an instructional vision incorporating technology, and
- the constraints of academic schedules and departmental structures.

Additional potential barriers to technology use that might be expected to play larger roles in the urban settings within which we did our case studies are

- lack of student technology skills,
- low expectations for student decision making, and
- accountability pressures.

Lack of Technology Infrastructure

The most visible barrier to the integration of technology into instruction in urban schools is the lack of access to modern computers and high-speed Internet connections. At the time our case studies began, neither Chicago nor Detroit public schools had provided a workable infrastructure for instructional uses of technology on a districtwide basis. Although both districts have made strides fostered by E-rate subsidies since that time, the technology infrastructures available in the schools we studied came about largely through the initiative of those individual schools, often working in concert with external partners. Chicago Learning Technologies Officer Richard White characterized such schools as islands of early adoption—isolated efforts that preceded a coordinated district plan. All of this is changing rapidly, particularly in Chicago, where a combination of district initiative and strategic use of E-rate funds has had a dramatic impact on schools' technology infrastructure over the last several years (Carvin, 2000).

At the time of our case studies, however, Bogan was the only one of the urban high schools with all of its classrooms wired for the Internet. For the most part, outside of business and computing courses, high school students had access to technology in computer labs rather than in regular classrooms. Although labs are easier to set up and manage than are distributed technology resources, they are susceptible to separation from core academic activities. When teachers must schedule time in a lab and move their class physically to a different location, they appear to be less likely to give assignments requiring technology use (Becker, Ravitz, & Wong, 1999). The situation is more problematic when there are not enough labs to meet the demand and when labs are physically located at a distance from a teacher's classroom. This kind of access issue was clearly at work at several of the high schools in our sample—most notably Best Practice and Renaissance. Both schools had very limited equipment inventories, which were also rapidly aging. A teacher who wanted to make technology a part of a long-term, challenging assignment had to plan ahead, successfully compete for the available technology resources, and stick to the preplanned schedule because other teachers would have scheduled the computer lab for the remaining time slots.

Other schools in our case study sample were less severely restricted by inventory issues. Although all of the schools would have liked more, and more up-to-date, equipment and network configurations, Bogan, Von Steuben, and Murray-Wright all had multiple labs and a student:computer ratio of 8:1 or better. Mumford's situation was somewhat in between. Although it had more computer labs and technical support than Best Practice or Renaissance, until school year 2000–01, Mumford's early leadership as a technology demonstration school was not followed up with a steady upgrading and expansion of its equipment inventory and network infrastructure outside the Tech Center. Mumford in fact had the most adverse student:computer ratio (at 16:1) of any of the schools we studied. Even so, the large size of its Tech Center (with fifty computers) and cohesiveness among its staff resulted in fewer complaints about lack of access to the lab than were registered in some other schools that actually had better student:computer ratios. Table 8.1 presents some indices of the technology infrastructure for the schools in our study.

Urban schools like Mumford, Von Steuben, and Renaissance fall into a kind of no-man's land with respect to funding for technology. Unlike many more affluent suburban schools, they do not receive major funding for technology purchases either from district funds or from parent contributions. On the other hand, because their students are relatively advantaged and high-achieving in comparison to others in their districts, they do not receive the federal or state compensatory education funding that many other urban schools are able to direct toward technology purchases and support. They are also entitled to smaller E-rate discounts than schools with higher poverty levels. The lack of a regular supply of funds that can be used for technology purchase and implementation places a premium on the principals' commitment and skills. If technology is to take hold in these schools, it will require principals who are committed to the effort, creative in identifying funding sources, and skilled at negotiating partnerships, inspiring grantsmanship among their staff, and following up on the many arrangements and activities that go into putting technology in place.

TABLE 8.1. Technology Infrastructure Indices.

School	Best Practice	Chicago		Detroit			
		Urban		Suburban	Urban			Suburban
		Bogan Computer Technical	Von Steuben Metro Science	Glenbrook South	Mumford	Murray-Wright	Renaissance	West Bloomfield
Number of students	340	1,847	1,443	2,304	1,900	1,754	860	1,860
Percent free or reduced-price lunch	81	76	60	10	38	53[a]	16	3
Number of computers for student use	37	300	300	450	120	224	69	542
Student:computer ratio	9:1	6:1	5:1	5:1	16:1	8:1	12:1	3:1
Percent of student computers with Internet access	75	100	83	100	65	60	1	90
Students per computer with Internet access	12:1	6:1	6:1	5:1	24:1	13:1	96:1	4:1
Number of computer labs	1	8	7	15	4	7	2	10
Percent of classrooms with computers for student use	81	100[b]	20[c]	5[d]	12	6	9	30
Percent of classrooms with Internet access	65	100	0	100	7	5[e]	3	95

Note: Chicago data are for school year 1998–99 and Detroit data are for 1999–2000 unless otherwise noted.
[a] In 1998–99.
[b] All classrooms have a minimum of one computer for student use.
[c] This number does not include mobile computers and instructional use of Media Center and Writing Lab.
[d] With computers carts included, 10 percent of classrooms have computers on a given day.
[e] All classrooms scheduled to be wired by end of 1999–2000 school year through Next Day.

Technical Support

Getting the boxes and wires in place is a necessary but not sufficient step in providing teachers with reliable access to technology. Network connections go down, parts fail, and software needs to be upgraded. Technical support for the infrastructure is an ongoing need and only increases as the infrastructure gets larger and more complex. The schools in our case study sample varied markedly in the extent and nature of the technical support available to them. Bogan and Von Steuben were the best supported, each having multiple on-site staff responsible for both technical aspects of technology support and for helping teachers to integrate technology into their instruction. Generally, however, technical support was a major problem among our case study schools, and nonfunctioning equipment and network connections were a common experience. Murray-Wright and Mumford each had a staff member responsible for a particular lab but no on-site person devoted to troubleshooting and technical support throughout the building. Best Practice and Renaissance were even more severely strapped for technical support, both relying on an individual in a different role (lead teacher and math department head, respectively) to act as de facto technology coordinator for the school; neither school had an on-site person devoted to technical support. Murray-Wright, Mumford, Best Practice, and Renaissance all relied on external vendors, in some cases paid for through the district and in some cases through school funds, for technical support for larger problems. Mumford's principal expressed the school's frustration with this arrangement: "It [technical support] comes, but it doesn't come quickly enough and when you're talking about student achievement, you need to be ready all of the time." Mumford's experience of waiting more than three months to get a new server up and running was not atypical.

Teacher Discomfort with Technology

Teachers who are not comfortable with technology themselves are less likely to design and implement classroom activities in which their students use technology. Federal, state, and district policymakers all have made the preparation of teachers to use technology effectively a priority. Our case studies confirm the need for teacher professional development with respect to technology but suggest that the need is for something more than computer literacy or acquiring technology skills per se. Certainly we talked with some teachers who expressed trepidation concerning the use of technology either for their own purposes or with their students, but these teachers were in a minority and teacher computer phobia did not appear to be the major stumbling block to technology implementation.

Many more teachers were themselves comfortable with computers than used them in their teaching. Most of the younger teachers had used technology in college, and many older teachers had been introduced to technology by their adolescent or adult children. Many teachers knew how to use general applications programs, such as word processing, spreadsheets, and e-mail, for their own purposes (e.g., composing tests, tracking grades) but did not know of worthwhile uses of technology in teaching the particular subjects for which they were responsible. Many had a vague sense that there were some high-quality technology applications somewhere "out there" but felt too pressured by other demands to have the time to seek them out. Others did not believe that high-quality technology resources exist in their subject area. The implication of these observations is that providing teachers with generic training in how to use technology tools may be helpful but probably will be insufficient to bring about a major shift in their practice toward student-empowering uses of technology.

Lack of Instructional Vision Incorporating Technology

As suggested in the preceding discussion, absence of a vision of how technology could support their specific instructional goals was a bigger deterrent than lack of technology skills per se for teachers in our case study schools. Although at the elementary school level it appears possible to motivate technology use through articulation of a schoolwide general instructional vision (e.g., "engaged learning") that involves a role for technology, at the high school level departmental goals are more prominent. More concrete, specific explications of how technology can support student learning in specific subject areas (e.g., mathematics, foreign language, science) are needed. Even principals who are very technology savvy themselves and big supporters of technology use (as were a number of the principals in our sample) have difficulty articulating an instructional vision incorporating technology for each and every academic department. Principals can set the tone and provide professional development opportunities and incentives, but they are dependent on departmental leadership to think through and promote an understanding of the role technology can play in supporting learning in their subject areas.

Lack of Student Technology Skills

Outside of computing or business classes, the central purpose of high school classes is not one of imparting technology skills. Even when a piece of software may be useful in helping students acquire concepts in the subject area that is the focus of the class or may support more sophisticated research or publications in the subject area, teachers will be reluctant to incorporate the technology if the time required to teach students to use it is too large relative to the degree of enhancement it brings to learning in the subject area. If teachers can assume that students already know how to use spreadsheet or presentation software, incorporating those applications into assignments entails what is usually a manageable increment in the amount of time required. If, on the other hand, some or all of the students have to be taught how to use the application before they can use it for their assignment, many teachers understandably will judge technology's added value too small in relation to the amount of time it will require. Some case study teachers cited the relatively low level and unevenness of technology skills among their students as a reason for minimizing technology use in class.

Several of our case study schools in CPS and DPS as a district tried to address this issue by instituting a required basic technology class in the ninth or tenth grade.[1] However, the effectiveness of this course was hampered in the Detroit schools we visited by the obsolescence of the equipment available for the computer course. In all three of the Detroit case study schools, the computers in the course's classroom were incapable of running contemporary software. Many teachers in the school felt the computer course was inadequate to prepare students for the kinds of technology uses that could support learning in the academic subject areas.

Thus, because they cannot count on students having acquired technology skills either in prior grades or at home, urban high school teachers will often decide that the incorporation of technology into class assignments entails too great a cost in terms of time and effort relative to its benefits. Here is a subtle way in which preexisting inequalities between urban and suburban or low- and high-income student populations (in terms of technology exposure) quite naturally lead to a magnification of inequalities because high school subject area teachers cannot afford the time to teach technology as well as their content area. Consider the disadvantage this situation creates for students, such as those at Renaissance, who pursue an academically rich high school curriculum but lack opportunities to use technology tools in their school work. When Renaissance graduates go on to elite universities, they will be competing with students who have four or even eight years' experience supporting their academic work with a wide array of technology tools.

Scarcity of High-Quality Digital Content

The educational software market is a tough place to try to make a profit. (Mattel gave away the Learning Company, one of the largest educational software firms in the United States, because that company was costing the parent corporation close to a million dollars

[1]CPS instituted a required freshman class in technology in the 1999–2000 school year.

a day in losses.) The most commonly used software in schools is the office applications package that is bundled with computers. Although the large number of potential users of software for enhancing basic reading and mathematics skills helps to attract developers to the elementary education market despite the difficulties of selling into schools and districts, there are few attractions from a financial investor's standpoint in developing quality software for more specialized courses such as tenth-grade literature as taught in a specific state or district. As content standards have received greater emphasis in most states and localities, the fact that those standards diverge from place to place makes it even more difficult for software developers to turn a profit while addressing local needs. Putting instructional materials on the Web can circumvent some of the economic problems of software development and of tailoring content for small markets, and many organizations, universities, and companies are posting educational materials on the Web. But Internet offerings are disorganized, of uneven quality, and often difficult to find. In a 1999 teacher survey concerning use of digital content by *Education Week*, 69 percent of secondary teachers said it was "very" or "somewhat" difficult to find the kind of content they want for their classroom (Zehr, 1999). Although teachers associations, state departments of education, and others have attempted to evaluate digital content in different subject areas and provide guidance for teachers in selecting appropriate materials, many teachers are either unaware of resources they could use or do not wish to invest the time required to review candidate materials, even with the tools and recommendations provided by these organizations.

Academic Schedule and Departmental Structure Constraints

The previously described opportunity costs of devoting significant time to teaching students to use technology, and simply the additional time that technology use almost always requires, are particularly problematic at the high school level because at most schools instructional periods are just forty to fifty minutes in length. High school teachers feel pressured to shoehorn a tremendous amount of content into these time segments, making it difficult to incorporate any kind of extended research or laboratory activity. Further, when that activity is technology based, there is the time sink associated with getting everyone logged on to the system, locating files, and dealing with the other technical minutiae before getting down to work. Many high school teachers feel that technology use is simply not feasible in the short periods available to them.

Several of our case study schools used a block schedule that supported more sustained student activities. Teachers described the importance of having these longer time segments when involving students in technology-supported projects. At one of the schools, however, the block scheduling combined with a limited equipment inventory had unfortunate side effects. Although the longer class sessions made it possible to engage in extended inquiry including technology-based activities in a single day, the longer time blocks meant that there were fewer "slots" in any given week during which a teacher could schedule the lab. The fact that only a single computer lab was available to nineteen teachers meant that the available slots quickly filled up, and some teachers felt it was useless to try to schedule technology-based activities.

Low Expectations for Student Decision Making

In the introduction to this volume we argued that even when the technology infrastructure in schools serving low-income students is equal to that in schools with more affluent student bodies, the kinds of experiences students have with technology are often different. Teachers with lower-income or lower-achieving students are more likely to use technology as a medium for providing drill and practice rather than for the kinds of student-centered uses of technology described above. The schools chosen for our case studies were selected as urban schools where low expectations are *not* the norm—

some of them have been recognized nationally for their high academic standards. Nevertheless, we did observe instances in which the use of technology was not associated with complex tasks and student direction of their own work. Rather, what appeared to be a customary teaching style of giving students step-by-step instructions and little latitude for reasoning or making choices was carried over to technology-based activities.

In one such class students were exploring occupations using an occupational inventory program on a CD-ROM in preparation for making PowerPoint slides. Students were told what occupations to research and, having chosen one for their presentation, exactly what information to include on each slide. Similarly, students in another class who were doing Internet research on various countries were told explicitly not only what information to obtain for each country but were given the URLs to use to find that information. In such classrooms students are using technology tools, but they are not having the experience of deciding when to use what tools, deciding what content is relevant to their purpose and appropriate for the audience of their work, or experimenting with technology's affordances. Such overdirected uses of technology were not the norm in the schools in our case study sample, but they did occur often enough to strike a cautionary note. We cannot assume that simply because technology is used in a class that the content of the instructional activity is interesting and challenging or even that the student is getting the essential skills for using technology in the real world (since these skills include the decision making and regulation that teachers are doing for their students).

Accountability Pressures

Over the past five years, the pressure on schools to be accountable for student learning, as demonstrated through student performance on mandated tests, has increased dramatically. Such pressures are particularly strong in districts that are perceived as failing and have motivated state takeover and replacement of the school superintendent with a CEO in both Chicago and Detroit. Because the kinds of learning supported by what we have called student-empowering uses of technology are so different from the factual knowledge and basic skills emphasized on tests used for accountability, many observers have noted a tension between technology use and the goal of improving test scores (Means, Penuel, & Quellmalz, 2000). Chicago Technology Resource Network (TRN) members, for example, noted that technology is a hard sell in schools worried about getting their test scores up high enough to avoid takeover. Schools often find themselves responding to what appear to be contradictory pressures. In Chicago, for example, they have state "engaged learning" goals with explicit encouragement to use technology to support attaining those goals, but at the same time they must meet standards for scores on basic skills tests or risk losing their jobs. Rockman (2000) goes so far as to assert "urban school districts have become schizophrenogenic, sending a variety of incompatible messages to teachers that result in confusion, misunderstanding, and often a return to earlier modes of behavior" (pp. 30–31).

Nevertheless, we did not find accountability pressures seriously undermining technology use in our case study schools in any direct way. In part, this lack of observed conflict may reflect the fact that most of the schools we studied performed well enough on standardized tests to escape district scrutiny. As Richard White, the CPS learning technologies officer put it, "Local school councils are demanding technology implementation in their schools. . . . If scores are not diving, and you [a principal] are bringing technology into the building, you are probably safe."

Teachers did not express a need to take students off technology-based activities in order to have them do something else perceived as more likely to raise their standardized test scores. A number of teachers expressed a more specific hypothesis concerning technology's positive contribution to test performance. They had found through experience that students are more engaged with technology-based activities. For this reason, they chose to incorporate technology into units on content that is stressed in their district's accountability system but not particularly engaging in its own right. Hence, technology became the carrot to attract students to learning about these topics.

Beating the Odds: Student-Empowering Uses of Technology in Urban High Schools

The preceding discussion of barriers to meaningful incorporation of technology is meant to provide a dose of realism but not despair. Despite all the difficulties and conflicting pressures, there are teachers in the high schools we studied who provide their students with challenging learning opportunities supported by technology. We turn now to a discussion of the elements in place in these teachers' classrooms and in their schools and districts that supported such model practices.

Like other instructional activities, technology-supported activities are highest in quality when they begin with a set of learning goals and with careful thought about the kinds of activities that will support attainment of those goals. Technology is best thought of as a means to an end rather than an end in itself. The best classroom activities had a driving purpose beyond the provision of technology use experience.

Despite the emphasis in the policy arena in providing teachers with formal professional development, district-provided technology training was not the inspiration for most of the exemplary classroom activities we observed. Rather, these teachers derived inspiration from their network of content experts in their teaching subject area. National associations and partnerships with university groups were a source of ideas and support for teaching challenging content and skills in science, writing, and mathematics. These teaching approaches happened to involve the use of technology, but technology was clearly a means rather than an end.

This is not to say that the only important form of professional development for technology use occurs outside the school. School-based professional development was very important also, particularly for those teachers not actively involved in external associations and partnerships. For these latter teachers, face-to-face interaction with colleagues they know and trust is the most effective strategy for influencing their practice. The extent to which these interactions occur constitutes the overall climate of collaboration within the school. Schools vary markedly in the extent to which teacher collaboration is supported by the administration and the extent to which it is a norm among teachers. Von Steuben and Mumford, for example, both had principals who placed a strong emphasis on collaboration among teachers and who understood that the process of collaboration is in fact professional development. The collaboration of teachers within Von Steuben's Writing Center and Mumford's Tech Center are emblematic of how professional development can be embedded into school activities and how a focus on academic content can be intimately connected with facilitation of technology use. Such examples help explain the recent survey finding (Becker, 1998) that teachers in schools where there is extensive communication and collaboration among the teaching staff are more likely to have their students use the Internet.

Points of Comparison: Technology Supports in Suburban High Schools

To help put the barriers and supports for technology use in urban high schools into perspective, the research team visited two suburban high schools in the same metropolitan areas. We briefly discuss the nature of technology supports and use in these high schools here, not to suggest that the suburban infrastructure and practices are necessarily ideal, but rather to try to explore some of the more subtle ways in which urban and suburban schools differ in the challenges they face in integrating technology. Table 8.1 provides indices of the technology infrastructures of the suburban schools in counterpoint to those in the urban case study sites. Our analysis will suggest that policies directed at the most obvious differences—differences in connectivity and amount of equipment—will leave important sources of inequality untouched.

Glenbrook South High School

A high school of 2,308 students in a well-to-do suburb of Chicago, Glenbrook South was an early technology adopter. In 1981 a Glenbrook South math teacher arranged for the purchase of a set of computers. Rather than using them exclusively for mathematics, the school placed the computers in an "Apple Orchard" within the social studies resource center and invited all the teachers to develop lesson plans incorporating technology. Based on teacher interest and planned uses, computers were moved from the lab to individual teachers' classrooms as new computers were purchased. The district superintendent, some board members, and several Glenbrook teachers undertook a tour of colleges to learn how technology was being used in teaching at the postsecondary level. In 1989 they undertook a systematic technology infrastructure building program, committing $1 million a year for five years to set up technology labs within the high school. Alan November, a nationally recognized educational technology consultant, served as the district's technology consultant from 1990 to 1994 and helped Glenbrook South staff think through their instructional goals for technology and derive their technology plan from those goals.

Glenbrook South has a main computer lab, the Titan Tech Center, and five departmental labs with assigned staff (devoted to mathematics, social studies, writing, computer graphics and keyboarding, and programming). Seven additional minilabs are available as alternative classrooms for special education, science, language, debate, newspaper, ESL, photography, and Title I. Each classroom has a teacher workstation and many have other computers, at the teacher's option. The school's LAN supported by fiber optic cable connects all computers, giving them access to the Internet through the school's T-1 line.

Glenbrook South's coordinator of instructional technology devotes 80 percent of his time to administering all of the technology areas within the school. He also acts as liaison to the district for technology. There are three technical support staff for the Titan Tech Center, including a network administrator and a network technician. Six support staff work in the five departmental computer labs. These staff members combine subject area and technical skills. The math lab supervisor, for example, is a math major with technical skills. The writing lab is staffed by two support staff, one technical and one an English major with technical skills.

As technology use within Glenbrook South has matured, it has continued to get strong district support. The school has received $250,000 annually for new computer purchases plus budget allotments for software, networking, and administrative software. All of the administrative, technical, and instructional support staff needed for the school's labs as well as the network maintenance staff are part of the regular budget.

Technology use is well integrated with instruction through much of the school. The Physics Department has an extensive Web page with student resources for research, practice quizzes, and keeping track of assignments. Simulation software is used heavily in physics as well as other courses within the Science Department. The Mathematics Department uses Mathematica, a symbolic computing program, graphing calculators, Excel spreadsheets, StatExplorer, Geometer's Sketchpad, and GeoExplorer. In addition to the common practice of using word processing for composing, the English department uses on-line threaded discussions of literature.

Staff development around technology use currently focuses on preparing teachers to provide on-line courses via the World Wide Web.

West Bloomfield High School

West Bloomfield High School is one of ten schools in an affluent school district on Detroit's northern fringe. Ninety percent of the graduates from this high school of 1,882 students go directly on to postsecondary education. With 121 teachers, the school has a student:teacher ratio of 16:1.

West Bloomfield was slower than Glenbrook South to make technology integration a priority. The press for technology use came initially from two departments—science and business. In the early 1990s West Bloomfield's Business Department was threatened with extinction in the face of declining enrollments and the press of additional academic requirements for graduation. Business teachers responded by modernizing their approach, bringing in new software programs and equipment. Current course offerings include CISCO Networking and Advanced Placement Computers as well as accounting, marketing, law, and business math courses that incorporate technology.

The Science Department also embarked on technology integration in the early 1990s. They obtained funding from a bond issue that they used to purchase twenty-four computers on a cart as a mobile lab. Housed in the department, the mobile lab could be moved from classroom to classroom as the need arose. They also obtained science simulation software for use with the mobile lab.

In 1993 the district superintendent took up the technology integration banner. He began an "every teacher will have a computer" campaign, offering every teacher in the district the opportunity to obtain a computer for his or her personal use in exchange for an agreement to complete seventy hours of technology training.

In 1996 West Bloomfield made a major investment in technology, creating a "technology wing" consisting of the "Criss Cross Lab" plus content area classrooms with multiple computers. In addition, the high school has six other labs (language, computer art, computer department, personal computing, and media center) plus a mobile wireless LAN of thirty-two laptops. Every classroom has at least one Internet-connected computer and a printer, and each of the labs has twenty or more multimedia workstations. The school's LAN is supported by single-strand fiber optic cable, and Internet access is provided through cable modem connections.

A variety of support staff keep the technology working and support teachers' use of it. Two "technology coaches" provide instructional support in the use of software and hardware. They conduct computer training classes that can be used to fulfill the requirement for obtaining a free computer from the district. One of the coaches also serves as a paratech for the building, troubleshooting hardware and software problems. Several "MediaTechs," assigned to the Media Center, provide on-site technical support for the Smartboard and audiovisual technologies located there. The district supplements this site-based technical support with two rotating technicians who handle maintenance and repairs for networks, computers, and peripherals in all ten of the district's schools, and an instructional technology systems coordinator, who works with the high school's MediaTechs to manage the video broadcast network, oversee the installation and repair of equipment, and conduct in-service training.

The district superintendent's support for technology is strong. Most recently he has introduced a capital improvement bond issue, "Clicks, Arts, and Mortar," which includes $52 million to upgrade technology in the district's ten schools over the next four years. In school year 1999–2000 the superintendent mandated teacher use of the district electronic mail system for communications. The district's Benchmarks for Learning outline specific grade-level standards for students in seven broad areas of technology integration and mastery.

Nearly 80 percent of the school's teachers have received technology training through the free computer for training program. Estimates of the proportion of West Bloomfield's teachers regularly using technology in instruction range from 50 to 80 percent. As a visitor moves from class to class, student use of technology appears widespread. Ninth graders in language arts classes use PowerPoint to create tutorials regarding different facets of South African life and culture. In biology class, students work with simulations of cell division presented on CD-ROM and conduct Web searches on related topics. In physics class, students use Excel to make graphs depicting their families' yearly gas and electricity use. Technical support teachers help the students import the graphs to a word processing program in which they write text analyzing the data and developing hypotheses to explain usage differences. In social studies class, students engage in on-line character play simulations, acting out the role of real-life politicians in Web-based "policy conferences."

The school's use of technology is embedded in a broader reform context. Two years ago, West Bloomfield adopted block scheduling to support more complex, authentic, hands-on learning activities. Technology is one of three overarching themes (writing and respect for diversity being the other two) that West Bloomfield is trying to integrate into every department.

Advantages of Suburban Schools

The majority of student uses of technology in the two suburban high schools were similar to those observed in urban schools. In both settings students performed Internet searches, created PowerPoint presentations, used word processing and desktop publishing, and used simulations to study science. Some technology uses in the suburban schools, however, were more cutting edge in nature: course activities organized around a complex Web site, on-line forums, and threaded discussions. Such practices are similar to activities being implemented in an increasing number of college courses. For a complex set of reasons, the suburban schools are better positioned to support cutting-edge technology applications.

Many teachers at the urban schools are similar to their suburban counterparts in terms of their instructional goals, but there is a striking difference not just in the nature of the technology infrastructure in the two sets of schools but in the extent to which teachers can count on the infrastructure they have to function. The technology plans in urban schools are not that different from those in suburbia—LANs with access to the Internet, departmental computer labs convenient to classes, modern multimedia-capable computers. But where the suburban schools have benefited from major bond issues and district support for building and maintaining the infrastructure described in their plans, urban schools have needed to scramble for funding that can never be taken for granted from year to year.

The teacher computer-for-training program illustrates how programs with similar goals play out under these differing financial circumstances. One of the urban case study high schools—Bogan—had an arrangement to give teachers a free computer if they agreed to either take or give technology classes, in essence the same program in place at West Bloomfield. But the difference is that whereas Bogan's principal had to wheel and deal to obtain twenty-four laptops with which to start the program, the computer-for-teachers program at Bloomfield is a districtwide initiative that has been in place for six years. Instead of scrambling for funds and hoping that the pieces will fit together, principals in suburban districts like Glenbrook and West Bloomfield can anticipate a level of adequacy and consistency in technology funding. Technology support positions are both more numerous and more established as business as usual. If an unexpected technical difficulty arises or an external partner does not come through with all the pieces needed to make a new computer lab fully operational, the district has the wherewithal to fill in the gaps.

Suburban schools also enjoy advantages in terms of the working environment they can provide to staff, the level of qualifications they can require in their teaching staff, and the culture of spending extra time on school activities that is more widely entrenched in suburban than in urban schools. Even when salary levels are equivalent, many teachers find suburban schools to be less stressful teaching environments. Newer buildings, more amenities near the school, and fewer discipline problems make suburban settings attractive. Perhaps partly as a result of these better working conditions, teachers in suburban schools appear less likely to point to the letter of the union-negotiated contract when asked to participate in professional development activities or serve on school committees. Given the amount of extra work that the introduction of technology into teaching and learning requires, this flexibility and willingness to contribute time on the part of teachers is a big advantage in the suburban setting.

In their study of urban high school reform efforts in the 1980s, Louis and Miles (1990) point to the potentially disruptive and divisive influences of the urban political environment. Urban schools are more likely to have to respond to mandates or challenges from the courts, community special interest groups, and militant unions. The school is less likely to be viewed as a community resource and social center and more likely to become embroiled in local political battles. (The demonstrations in Detroit after the state wrested control of the schools from the locally elected school board were a vivid example of this problem during the period of our case studies.)

Another difference we observed was the source of leadership for technology integration. In the large urban districts where we did our case studies, strong commitment and involvement on the principal's part appear necessary to bring technology into the school. Districts play supporting roles, but the principals have to actively negotiate with their districts around their needs and to act as promoters with their own teachers. They lead the school in finding external partners and grant opportunities that can support technology purchase and integration. They use the time and dollar resources available to them in flexible ways that support the infusion of technology. Although we visited just two suburban high schools, the difference in the source of leadership for technology use was suggestive. In both suburban cases much of the impetus for technology use came from the district superintendent, whose push for technology funding and instructional uses of technology made it possible for individual teachers to spearhead technology integration efforts within their departments. The principals in suburban schools did not have to be leaders in the technology integration efforts for those efforts to succeed. Superintendents, on the other hand, played a stronger role in the suburban schools' technology initiatives.

We do not believe that urban superintendents are antitechnology or unaware of the importance of equipping their students to use new technologies to support their learning and their work. Urban superintendents simply are likely to be working in crisis mode, try-ing to restore basic public confidence in their school systems. When serious questions arise about whether a district's schools can teach students to read, developing a new vision of technology integration is not likely to be the district's top priority. (During the 1999–2000 school year there were indications that as confidence in the CPS system has risen, the district CEO, Paul Vallas, has started to place more emphasis on instructional uses of technology.) In addition to their greater public support and stability, the suburban districts are much smaller than the urban districts, and size does make a differ-ence. Suburban superintendents are likely to have much closer con-nections with the staffs of individual high schools, simply because they have many fewer with which to deal.

Louis and Miles (1990) argue that large urban districts, with their large, departmentalized bureaucracies and press to cope with both local political pressures and state and federal policies, tend to treat all the schools within their jurisdiction as if they are the same. This district orientation, Louis and Miles assert, places heavy demands on the urban school principal: "The principal, if he or she is to be effective, must be simultaneously a supreme politician, negotiating special resources and exemptions from 'the rules,' and an outlaw who is willing to spend time covering up unauthorized deviations from policy" (pp. 13–14).

Recommendations

Our case studies suggest that the picture of technology integration in urban high schools is a complex one—that exciting and empow-ering instructional uses of technology are happening in some class-rooms and some schools but that such applications are nowhere near as frequent as one would wish. On the one hand, many urban schools are woefully ill-equipped with respect to computers and net-work access; on the other hand, many schools are not making good use of the resources they have. Based on our Detroit and Chicago case studies and on our research on technology-supported reform efforts throughout the country, we offer recommendations for districts, high schools, and teachers.

Actions for Districts

Offer stable, flexible support for school technology infrastructures. The comparison between urban and suburban high schools suggests that one of the major advantages suburban schools enjoy with respect to technology implementation is the greater consistency and stability of district supports from year to year. Technology for instructional purposes is still a relatively new part of district budgets, and economically strapped urban districts find it difficult to locate and earmark funds for technology on a recurring basis. Although we are fully aware of the difficulty of doing so, we encourage urban school districts to seek funds for technology and to think about technology expenses as businesses do, as regular recurring expenses rather than special, onetime purchases. Having some sense of the support they can expect from their districts and a belief that the support will be ongoing gives schools a reason to believe that their efforts in technology planning and teacher training will not be wasted.

Just as important as support for the technology box-and-cable infrastructure is the human technical support to get and keep the technology up and running. Lack of timely technical support was a serious problem in the majority of the urban case study schools. Although a few of the schools had found the resources to support not just one but multiple on-site technicians to support their technology, other case study schools had no dedicated technology coordinator position and instead relied on an individual assigned to another role to fill this function as an added responsibility. A Spring 1999 survey of Chicago high schools by The Chicago Panel suggests that this spotty availability of on-site technical assistance is typical: Just ten of seventeen Chicago high schools responding to the survey had technology coordinator positions. Any high school making serious use of computers and the Internet should have an on-site technical support person.

In addition to stability in support for technology purchases and maintenance, urban school districts would do well to look for places where flexibility in the nature of the support offered can make more effective use of funds. Although treating all schools within a district uniformly is less open to political challenge and has the advantage of ensuring at least some minimal level of support for everyone, it can leave individual schools with technology resources that do not fit their needs. Such policies result in anomalies such as tiny Best Practice High School with two T-1 lines and only thirty-seven computers. Several informants noted also that because of multiple federal and state programs providing funding on the basis of the number of students on free or reduced-price lunch, those urban schools with high poverty levels are getting significant amounts of funding either earmarked for or potentially used for technology while those urban schools with lower poverty levels are extremely limited in the discretionary funds available for technology and related staff development expenses. In recognition of this problem, CPS has recently set up a fund to support technology implementation in Chicago schools that do not qualify for high levels of compensatory education or E-rate funds. Another step districts can take is to encourage high school students to sign up for the federal lunch program if they are qualified. In many districts, including Detroit, the high school poverty rates, estimated on the basis of participation in the lunch program, are on the order of half those of the poverty rates of the elementary schools. It is unlikely that high school students come from more economically comfortable families than do the younger students, who are typically their siblings. Rather, there appears to be a disinclination among secondary students to participate in the school lunch program, a disinclination that districts can combat by explaining the importance of program participation for school funding.

Develop and implement balanced assessment systems. The disconnect between conventional large-scale assessments stressing factual knowledge and basic skills and the kinds of learning promoted by what we have called student-empowering uses of technology was noted earlier. Much of what students get taught is influenced by the nature of the tests on which teachers, schools, and districts are judged. If we want all students to have the opportunities to learn how to use technology as supports for analysis, understanding, and communication, we need to be able to demonstrate what they are learning from these experiences. Including measures of these skills in assessment programs will make teachers feel more comfortable devoting class time to technology-supported activities and will help clarify for teachers, students, and parents the nature of the advanced skills and understanding students can acquire using technology. Moreover, participation in the development and field testing of such assessments (along with individuals with expertise in performance assessment and test construction) can be a powerful form of teacher professional development (Lieberman, 1995).

Recognize and support a range of forms and sources of professional development involving technology. One of the major implications of our case studies is that much of teachers' learning occurs through informal, often one-on-one, interactions with colleagues. Organizational structures that support such interactions, through mechanisms such as Von Steuben's Writing Center or Mumford's Tech Center, should be recognized as valid forms of professional development worthy of district support and credit toward promotion and pay increases. Similarly, forms of summer institutes with follow-on through on-line teacher communities, such as Chicago's Technology Infusion Program (TIP), are promising.

Our experience in other parts of the country suggests that a community of technology-using teachers with supported time and incentives for working together can be a potent form of teacher support. A system of supports to foster and provide incentives for partnerships between more- and less-technology-proficient teachers *within* a school can be effective in spreading technology use (Penuel, Means, & Simkins, 2000). Across schools, a combination of face-to-face and electronic interaction, with access to outside sources of expertise regarding instructional uses of technology, and subject-based as well as geographically based subgroupings, would be most likely to succeed.

Another important lesson from the case studies is the importance of integrating technology into professional development in academic content areas at the secondary level. High school teachers associate themselves with their discipline and are held responsible for student learning in that specific subject. They need to see models of effective technology use in the subject areas they teach.

Support principals' learning about technology integration and how to develop external sources for technology funding. We have pointed repeatedly to the pivotal role of principals in bringing technology integration to their schools. Principals are required not only to know enough about technology to negotiate with vendors and potential equipment and service providers but also to have an instructional vision for technology use, a plan for promoting teacher learning about technology use, and the ability to identify and successfully pursue outside sources of funding and expertise to support technology in their schools. Few principals come equipped with all these skills, and districts should support principals' professional development just as they support that of teachers. CPS recently took a groundbreaking step in this direction in establishing the Administrators' Reform Community, featuring a series of workshops and on-line interactions bringing Chicago principals together with each other and with technology researchers to share insights and work through technology integration issues.

Provide incentives and recognition for integration of technology with the teaching of challenging content. As important as the financial and training supports that districts can offer schools is the simple fact of recognition. Finding ways to identify and honor teacher achievements in integrating technology with challenging content and the student accomplishments made possible by these teachers should be a priority. In the Silicon Valley Challenge 2000 Multimedia Project, annual student multimedia fairs have become an important tool for promoting students' use of technology, promulgating an instructional model that stresses student-empowering uses of technology, and bringing public recognition to the schools (Penuel, Means, & Simkins, 2000).

Actions for School Leadership

Make sure teachers have access to computers and the Internet for their own use. Teachers are more likely to use technology with their students if they themselves feel comfortable with technology and if they have good access to information about technology-based instructional resources. Providing teachers with technology access helps satisfy these conditions. Moreover, the provision of computers for their personal use is one of the most direct ways that a school can make teachers feel supported in their technology integration efforts. Laptop computers offer flexibility and the option for using technology at home as well as at school. Increasingly, schools are seeing value in supporting home Internet connections for their staff as well.

In cases where it is not feasible to provide every teacher with a take-home computer, schools can still support teachers by providing workspace with computers and other resources. There is value both in having private spaces where teachers can experiment with technology without fear of scrutiny and larger workspaces where they can use technology in a collaborative fashion while planning joint instructional activities or discussing technology-based tools and resources with colleagues.

Create opportunities for teachers to observe and learn from technology-proficient colleagues in their discipline. Like most of us, teachers prefer to learn from colleagues with whom they have extensive contact and a high level of comfort. Principals can foster situations in which teachers can learn informally from each other, through joint projects such as the Love and Marriage theme at Bogan or the Family Tree activities at Mumford, or through ongoing support roles such as Lucja Kowalski's leadership of the Writing Center at Von Steuben. By finding flexibility within the system to support joint planning time and staff members in "bridge" roles connecting technology to subject areas, principals and department heads can not only foster technology integration but also improve staff cohesion and school climate. This strategy requires identifying existing teachers with the right combination of subject matter expertise, technology skills, and consulting skills to support their colleagues or hiring new staff who can lead the integration of technology into existing departments.

Another component of this strategy is rewarding and supporting technology-using teachers with professional development experiences outside the school. Such activities expose teachers to new ideas, increase their sense of professional competence, and make them aware of approaches and resources they can use with their students and share with their colleagues.

Support teachers' development of technology integration ideas and then seek additional sources of funding from grants programs, business partners, and the school community. One of the striking features of the case study schools with the most successful technology integration was the conviction of staff at those schools that if they had a good idea for using technology with their students, their principal would find a way to support implementation of that idea. This kind of school climate does not arise by chance. Principals need to stage activities that encourage and invite teacher ideas for using technology and then to stimulate, and often lead, efforts to get the funding to support implementation of those ideas. Principals of successful technology-using schools negotiate with district offices for funds, lead grant-writing efforts, and deal with corporate partners willing to make donations or provide services. It is important that teachers with a strong commitment to student-empowering uses of technology have convenient access to the technology they need. Typically, funding sources are not earmarked for technology purchases per se. Grants are awarded to upgrade the science curriculum, offer a more student-friendly ninth-grade program, or enhance teachers' mathematics knowledge. Savvy principals identify the intersection between the purposes of the grant programs and the school's goals for using technology. They do not pursue funding opportunities or accept donations willy-nilly without considering whether the requirements for receiving funding or the donated equipment are consistent with the school's culture and instructional goals.

Consider block scheduling for at least a portion of the school week. Complex technology-supported projects take time. Longer instructional periods make this kind of work more feasible. Bogan and Best Practice used block scheduling at the time of our case studies, and Mumford was planning to adopt the plan.

Actions for Teachers

Reflect on those things that have proved most difficult to teach in the past, and consider whether technology could support student learning in these areas. For most classes, technology is a means to an end, not an end in itself. Given the time requirements and amount of effort required to use technology, it makes sense to employ this tool in those cases where students can reap the greatest benefits. Research suggests that in addition to its motivational advantage, technology can help students master abstract content (Roschelle et al., 2000) and acquire communication skills (National Research Council, 1999). The astronomy concepts students learn through Hands-on Universe at Best Practice and the practical problem solving in Stanley Henry's mathematics class at Murray-Wright are good examples of the selective use of technology.

Use the professional teaching organization in your subject area as a guide to technology-supported innovations, Web resources, and software that others in your field regard as exemplary. Learning about the integration of technology into instruction in one's teaching field is really simply one part of learning about new resources and instructional strategies. Organizations such as the National Science Teachers Association, the American Geographical Union, the National Council of Teachers of Mathematics, and the National Council of Teachers of English are good starting points for learning about digital content and curriculum projects that use technology in powerful ways. Web sites and conferences are important sources of information. They can serve as pointers both to powerful content and approaches and to teachers elsewhere who are implementing these programs. Although many teachers feel they are not "working" unless they are standing in front of a room full of students, observing others using promising technology materials or approaches is a legitimate and enriching part of professional development.

Team with a technology support person or another teacher when implementing complex technology-supported work. Most of the teachers we observed implementing complex, student-empowering uses of technology did so with the collaboration and support of a colleague at their school. Murray-Wright's Julie Oberly, for example, said she could not have done her African American Scientists Quilt project without the help of Katie Fitzner. At Von Steuben, science teachers Mary Jo Arnashus and Nancy Schlack developed their course units together and kept a cart with the current unit's technology-based resources available for rolling back and forth between their classrooms. Two teachers at Mumford relied on Claudia Burton to help them integrate use of the Family Tree Maker software into their units on the Harlem Renaissance and African American history. In our experience, many of the richest technology-supported classroom activities are both designed and implemented by a pair or small group of teachers rather than a teacher working solo (Means & Olson, 1995). Moreover, when both the content and the technology are complex, the presence of an extra adult can make all the difference in the smooth running of a class. At the most successful technology-using urban high schools, principals provide support for teacher joint work, and teachers go out of their way to work with and support each other.

Incorporate assessment into technology-supported classroom work; involve students in discussing and applying criteria for judging the quality of technology-based products. Technology, especially new technology, is exciting for teachers as well as students. Sometimes it is easy to get caught up in the excitement of the bells and whistles without stopping to think carefully about content—what is being learned. One of the best ways to avoid this pitfall (whether using technology or any other innovation) is to think carefully about how learning will be assessed before starting the project. By clarifying learning goals and how student work will be judged, teachers can keep their classes on track.

Many teachers have found it useful to involve their students in developing and applying criteria for judging the products of their technology-based work (Penuel & Means, 2000). Since the ultimate goal is to have students who can regulate their own learning, practice in developing and applying standards of quality is a highly useful skill as well as a technique for eliciting better work from students.

Model technology learning for your students, and gratefully accept student help. Many teachers who initially worried about introducing technology into their classes achieved a major sense of liberation upon realizing that they did not have to know everything about the technology themselves. Moreover, it is highly useful for students to observe how their teacher thinks and acts when confronting a technology question for which he or she does not have a ready answer. Observing their teacher's reasoning about the problem, willingness to try multiple approaches, and use of on-line help, documentation, and other people is valuable for students.

Especially at the high school level, students are often a significant source of technical assistance, as in Oni Akilah's digital art class at Renaissance. Schools can also develop programs to make systematic use of student technology expertise, as at Mumford's Tech Center and the Technology Club started by Randy Snow at Von Steuben. At these schools, students help maintain the computers and network and provide assistance to technology-using teachers as well as their fellow students.

The Digital Divide Revisited

In summarizing our observations of technology integration in urban and suburban high schools, we return to the issue characterized as the "digital divide." Is the introduction of technology into schools magnifying or minimizing existing differences in educational opportunity?

Urban high schools are making a strong effort to develop a technology infrastructure that will give their students the same kinds of tools and experiences suburban high school students enjoy. As much new technology and network capacity as urban schools are adding, however, more affluent districts remain on the whole several steps ahead. Becker (2000) argues that the standard for school technology infrastructure is a moving target, and the difference between the infrastructures in more and less affluent schools is most appropriately characterized in terms of the number of years less well supported schools will need to catch up. Becker estimates that, nationally, schools with large proportions of low-income students are one to two years behind those with enrollments drawn primarily from average-income families and that these schools are in turn one to two years behind schools in affluent areas such as South Glenbrook and West Bloomfield. Administrators responsible for low-income schools must feel the brunt of the old saying "It takes all the hurrying I can do just to stay in one place."

Although research has demonstrated the potential for technology to make complex and abstract content more accessible to a wide range of students (Roschelle et al., 2000), urban students are getting only limited exposure to the kinds of technology supports that have been shown to be effective in teaching science and mathematics concepts. Student-empowering uses of technology applications are appearing in urban high schools, as described in our case studies, but such uses of technology are more common in privileged high schools. Moreover, students from more affluent communities are more likely to have home access both to technology and to knowledgeable siblings and adults who can advise them on how to use it. Technology has the potential to be an equalizing force, but for the most part, that equalizing is not occurring. Given differences in home access and support, students in urban schools need not just equal but *better* access to technology and high-quality learning activities involving technology if they are to get to the same place as their peers in well-to-do suburban schools.

Some urban high schools, like Bogan, have taken up the mantle of teaching about technology per se. Recognizing the high demand for skilled staff in the technology industry, these schools have taken an unabashedly work-oriented view of their mission. They hope to produce graduates who have technology skills better matched to the workplace than the graduates of general or traditionally academic high schools. But the majority of urban high schools are more concerned with preparing students for college or a wide range of postsecondary experiences and will find it difficult to "leapfrog" the technology integration accomplishments of more privileged schools. To do so will require long-term commitment to budgetary support not just for wires and boxes but also for the support personnel who can keep them running and for experts who can work with teachers to identify and adapt or to devise effective uses of technology within their academic disciplines. Equally challenging, it will require kinds of incentives and professional development for teachers that thus far have been rare in public high schools. Teachers need exposure to new ideas and resources for using technology in their specific subject areas and supported time to assimilate these ideas into their own plans and practices. They need the opportunity to observe expert technology-using teachers in their subject area and the opportunity to try out new approaches and receive feedback on their initial efforts. All of this needs to unfold in an atmosphere where risk taking and innovation are encouraged and teacher professional growth is valued.

In addition to a system providing supports and incentives for this kind of professional growth, a culture of communication, collaboration, and working beyond required hours needs to be established in urban schools if they are to become accomplished at implementing student-empowering uses of technology. Thus, urban school systems will need to give more to their teachers, and a greater proportion of teachers will have to give more to their schools if all the investment in technology is to have the desired impacts. As shown in several of our case studies, those urban schools that have established a culture of collaboration, commitment, and experimentation have been able to do much in terms of meaningful integration of technology, despite all the challenges and constraints of urban education.

References

Anderson, R. E., & Ronnkvist, A. (1999). *The presence of computers in American schools*. Irvine, CA: Center for Research on Information Technology and Organizations.

Anderson, R. E., Welch, W. W., & Harris, L. J. (1984). Inequities in opportunities for computer literacy. *The Computing Teacher, 11*, 10–12.

Becker, H. J. (1998, April). *The influence of computer and internet use on teachers' pedagogical practices and perceptions*. Paper presented at the Annual Meeting of the American Educational Research Association, San Diego, CA.

Becker, H. J. (1999). *Internet use by teachers*. Irvine, CA: Center for Research on Information Technology and Organizations.

Becker, H. J. (2000). Who's wired and who's not: Children's access to and use of computer technology. *The Future of Children, 10*, 44–75.

Becker, H. J., Ravitz, J., & Wong, Y. (1999). *Teacher and teacher-directed student use of computers and software*. Irvine, CA: Center for Research in Information Technology and Organizations.

Carvin, A. (2000). Mind the gap: The Digital Divide as the civil rights issue of the new millennium. *Multimedia Schools, 7*. http://www .infotoday.com/MMSchools/Jan00/carvin.htm.)

Cuban, L. (1986). *Teachers and machines: The classroom uses of technology since 1920*. New York: Teachers College Press.

Education Writers of America. (1999). *Barriers and breakthroughs: Technology in urban schools*. Washington, DC: Author.

Greene, D., David, J. L., & Young, V. (2000). *Strategic review of professional development services provided by the Learning Technologies Office of the Chicago Public Schools*. Palo Alto, CA: Bay Area Research Group.

Heath, S. B., & McLaughlin, M. (1993). *Identity and inner city youth*. New York: Teachers College Press.

Hess, F. M. (1999a). A political explanation of policy selection: The case of urban school reform. *Policy Studies Journal, 27*, 459–473.

Hess, F. M. (1999b). The state role in school reform: A local perspective. *Planning and Changing, 30*, 43–52.

Hess, G. A., Jr. (1999). Understanding achievement (and other) changes under Chicago school reform. *Education and Policy Analysis, 21* (1), 67–83.

Honey, M., Carrigg, F., & Hawkins, J. (1998). *Union city online: An architecture for networking and reform. Learning with technology: The 1998 yearbook of the Association for Supervision and Curriculum Development*. Alexandria, VA: Association for Supervision and Curriculum Development.

Honey, M., & Culp, K. M. (2000). The E-rate in practice: Research findings from four midwestern cities. In N. A. Carvin (Ed.), *The E-rate in America: A tale of four cities* (pp. 16–25). Newton, MA: Benton Foundation.

International Society for Technology in Education (ISTE). (1998). *National educational technology standards for students*. Eugene, OR: Author.

Keller, B. (1998, May 6). Report calls for decentralization of Detroit school administration. *Education Week*.

Lee, V. E., Smith, J. B., & Croninger, R. G. (1995). *Another look at high school restructuring: More evidence that it improves student achievement, and more insight into why. Issues in Restructuring Schools, Issue Report #9* (pp. 1–10). Madison, WI: Wisconsin Center for Education Research, University of Wisconsin.

Lieberman, A. (1995). Practices that support teacher development. *Phi Delta Kappan, 76*, 591–596.

Louis, K. S., & Miles, M. B. (1990). *Improving the urban high school: What works and why*. New York: Teachers College Press.

Means, B. (1994). Introduction: Using technology to advance educational goals. In B. Means (Ed.), *Technology and education reform: The reality behind the promise* (pp. 1–21). San Francisco: Jossey-Bass.

Means, B., Blando, J., Olson, K., Middleton, T., Morocco, C. C., Remz, A. R., & Zorfass, J. (1993). *Using technology to support education reform.* Washington, DC: U.S. Government Printing Office.

Means, B., & Golan, S. (1998). *Transforming teaching and learning with multimedia technology.* San Jose, CA: Joint Venture: Silicon Valley Network.

Means, B., & Olson, K. (1994). Tomorrow's schools: Technology and reform in partnership. In B. Means (Ed.), *Technology and education reform: The reality behind the promise* (pp. 191–222). San Francisco: Jossey-Bass.

Means, B., & Olson, K. (1995). *Technology's role for education reform: Findings from a national study of innovating schools.* Washington, DC: U.S. Department of Education.

Means, B., Penuel, W. R., & Quellmalz, E. (2000, September). *Developing assessments for tomorrow's classrooms.* Paper presented at the Secretary's Conference on Educational Technology 2000, Washington, DC.

Moll, L. C., Amanti, C., Neff, D., & Gonzalez, N. (1992). Funds of knowledge for teaching: Using a qualitative approach to connect homes and classrooms. *Theory into Practice, 31,* 132–141.

Moore, G. (1991). *Crossing the chasm: Marketing and selling technology products to mainstream customers.* New York: Harper Business.

National Center for Education Statistics (NCES). (2000). *Internet access in U.S. public schools and classrooms: 1994–1999.* (NCES No. 2000086). Washington, DC: U.S. Government Printing Office.

National Council for Geographic Education. (1994). *Geography for life: National geography standards.* Indiana, PA: Author.

National Louis University. (1997). Best Practice High School: Extending NCE's progressive tradition. *National College of Education Quarterly, 19,* 1, 1–4.

National Research Council. (1999). *How people learn: Brain, mind, experience, and school.* Washington, DC: National Academy Press.

President's Committee of Advisors on Science and Technology. (1997). *Report to the President on the use of technology to strengthen K-12 education in the United States.* President's Committee of Advisors on Science and Technology: Panel on Educational Technology. Washington, DC: Author.

Penuel, W. R., Means, B., & Simkins, M. (2000). The multimedia challenge. *Educational Leadership, 58,* 34–38.

Penuel, W. R., & Means, B. (2000, April). *Designing a performance assessment to measure student communication skills in multimedia-supported project-based learning.* Paper presented at the Annual Meeting of the American Educational Research Association, New Orleans, LA.

Poe, J. (1996, September 15). Adventures in education: Concept focuses on small schools. *Chicago Tribune.*

Rockman, S. (2000). *Technology, urban school reform and the schizophrenic nature of teaching.* Briefing paper prepared for the meeting Technology's Role in Urban School Reform: Achieving Equity and Quality, sponsored by the Joyce Foundation, the Center for Children and Technology, and the Johnson Foundation.

Rockman et al. (2000). *A more complex picture: Laptop use and impact in the context of changing home and school access.* San Francisco: Author.

Roschelle, J., Pea, R., Hoadley, C., Gordin, D., & Means, B. (2000). Changing how and what children learn in school with computer-based technologies. *The Future of Children, 10,* 76–101.

Rosenfeld, H. (1991). Commentary on "A Cognitive Apprenticeship for Disadvantaged Students." In B. Means, M. Knapp, & C. Chelemer (Eds.), *Teaching advanced skills to at-risk students* (pp. 244–254). San Francisco: Jossey-Bass.

Snyder, T. (2000, August). Remarks before a National Research Council meeting, the Digital Divide and Digital Democracy, Menlo Park, CA.

The Auto Channel. (1997, July). Lear Corporation receives Ford Motor Company Corporate Citizen Award. [On-line]. Available: http://www.theautochannel.com/news/press/date/19970721/press004 308.html.

The Chicago Panel. (1999). *Reform report.* Chicago, IL: Author.

U.S. Department of Education. (1999, September). *Annual back-to-school address: Changing American high school to fit modern times.* Remarks prepared for delivery by U.S. Secretary of Education Richard W. Riley to The National Press Club. [On-line]. Available: http://www .ed.gov/Speeches/09-1999/990915.html.

Wenglinsky, H. (1998). *Does it compute? The relationship between educational technology and student achievement in mathematics.* Princeton, NJ: Educational Testing Service.

Zehr, M. A. (1999, September). Is the software right for you? Technology Counts '99 [On-line]. Available: http://www.edweek.org/sreports/tc99 /articles/screening-s1.htm.

Index